Praise for *The Girl in the Orange Dress*

"With this book, Margot Starbuck unleashes her new, very welcome, voice. She narrates the Christian spiritual life with winsome humor and (occasionally scary) honesty. Pretty much every woman I know will be getting *The Girl in the Orange Dress* for her birthday."
LAUREN F. WINNER, author of *Girl Meets God*

"Outrage, grief, joy and humor mingle together in Margot Starbuck's book, drawing the reader into her experiences in a way that leaves one feeling neither like judge nor voyeur, just a friend on the journey. Humbly honest, graciously hilarious, evocative, *The Girl in the Orange Dress* is for anyone who needs to know, really needs to know, how much God loves his children."
LISA SAMSON, award-winning author of *Quaker Summer, Justice in the Burbs* and *The Church Ladies*

"Margot Starbuck takes us on a lovely and challenging journey, searching for herself, her family and her faith along the way."
SHAUNA NIEQUIST, author of *Cold Tangerines*

"Will this book be made into a movie? A TV series? A graphic novel? Well, it oughta. Margot Starbuck's story has legs, and it'll captivate anyone who has a chance to hear it, in whatever way they can. Her easygoing style spins this unique yarn into an every(wo)man tale that can speak to us all."
PATTON DODD, senior editor, Beliefnet.com, and author of *My Faith So Far*

"A lovely journey through family, failure and friendships to finally find a Father who does not fail. Sure to charm and challenge all spiritually minded seekers and sojourners."
PATRICIA RAYBON, author of *I Told the Mountain to Move*

"The desire for a father who sees, knows, hears and loves us is the quintessential longing in every girl's heart. In *The Girl in the Orange Dress*, Margot Starbuck chronicles her own search for a Father who doesn't fail her, and the good news is she lands us right in the heart of God: the one who accepts us and never fails us. Thank you, Margot, for sharing your journey and reminding us once again that he is the only one that can truly fill our longing for 'perfect' on earth."
JENNIFER STRICKLAND, speaker and author of *Girl Perfect: Confessions of a Former Runway Model* (www.jenniferstrickland.net)

"This is a story hard to put down. It is a fascinating read. Margot's ability to capture the essence of the search—not just for her biological father, but ultimately for her heavenly Father—is intriguing, unique and most of all real. Throughout the book, I felt like a fellow traveler, quietly joining in her journey . . . encouraging her on. This book is a must-read for anyone who might find themselves on a similar search—one of a lifetime."
JAYNE SCHOOLER, author of *The Whole Life Adoption Book*

"Starbuck gets it—what many fail to understand about how much it hurts to lose your parents at birth. Being relinquished, that is, given away, and then taken by others can be a core injury to the developing human heart. . . . Delightfully written, this autobiography is a great read for those who want to understand more about the agony of abandonment and the joy of belonging."
RONALD NYDAM, Ph.D., author of *Adoptees Come of Age*

THE GIRL IN THE
ORANGE DRESS

Searching for a father who does not fail

MARGOT STARBUCK

IVP Books
An imprint of InterVarsity Press
Downers Grove, Illinois

InterVarsity Press
P.O. Box 1400, Downers Grove, IL 60515-1426
World Wide Web: www.ivpress.com
E-mail: email@ivpress.com

InterVarsity Press® is the book-publishing division of InterVarsity Christian Fellowship/USA®, a movement of students and faculty active on campus at hundreds of universities, colleges and schools of nursing in the United States of America, and a member movement of the International Fellowship of Evangelical Students. For information about local and regional activities, write Public Relations Dept., InterVarsity Christian Fellowship/USA, 6400 Schroeder Rd., P.O. Box 7895, Madison, WI 53707-7895, or visit the IVCF website at <www.intervarsity.org>.

Scripture quotations, unless otherwise noted, are from the New Revised Standard Version of the Bible, copyright 1989 by the Division of Christian Education of the National Council of the Churches of Christ in the USA. Used by permission. All rights reserved.

While all the stories in this book are true, some names and identifying details have been changed to protect the privacy of the people involved.

Published in association with the literary agency of WordServe Literary Group, Ltd., 10152 Knoll Circle, Highlands Ranch, CO 80130.

Design: Cindy Kiple
Cover image: Diego Uchitel/Getty Images
Interior images: Shutterstock
Author photo: Scott Faber

ISBN 978-0-8308-3627-7

Printed in the United States of America ∞

Library of Congress Cataloging-in-Publication Data

Starbuck, Margot, 1969-
 The girl in the orange dress: searching for a father who does not
 fail / Margot Starbuck.
  p. cm.
 ISBN 978-0-8308-3627-7 (pbk.: alk. paper)
 1. Starbuck, Margot, 1969- 2. Christian biography—United States.
 I. Title.
 BR1725.S734A3 2009
 277.3'0825092—dc22
 [B]
                                                                2009011826

P   18   17   16   15   14   13   12   11   10   9   8   7   6   5   4   3   2   1

Y   24   23   22   21   20   19   18   17   16   15   14   13   12   11   10   09

Thank you, Sweet P, for being for me.

In the place where it was said to them,

"You are not my people,"

it shall be said to them,

"Children of the living God."

HOSEA 1:10

CONTENTS

- one -

MY PERFECT CHILDHOOD

"I just loved you immediately. You were adorable, just adorable. I looked at you, and you were my daughter." My adoptive mother's eyes still sparkle and tear up as she describes her first glimpse of me at a Boston adoption agency. In my mind I see her taking me in her arms, looking into my eyes, and thinking that I am the most beautiful little baby girl she has ever seen.

"I had gotten you a little white dress with blue satin ribbon on it," she continues. "The first thing I did was to change you out of that orange outfit."

Numb

We moved to a suburb of Chicago when I was two. The rounded yellow door of our Tudor-style brick house at 733 Pine Avenue was framed by rugged stones and climbing ivy. For some mysterious reason, we never owned a key to that stately door. We just always went in and out the plain back door.

Someone from the local chamber of commerce with an eye for charm had actually snapped a photo of the house from the street when we weren't looking. It was featured on the cover of a countywide real estate magazine. The fact that our home had been selected to represent the area pleased me. The view from the curb confirmed it: we were the perfect family in the perfect home in the perfect town.

When I was five, however, my father accepted a job on the East Coast, in Connecticut. He began working there while my mother, my brother and I remained behind. Though the extended absence was ostensibly for business, on one of his visits home, he and my mother gathered my eleven-year-old brother, Scott, and me together to tell us they were divorcing. I was six years old.

Our parents said all the right words. They didn't trouble us with adult matters, like my father's alcoholism. They assured us that we were loved. The news of their divorce, though, was simply not emotional information I could process. I didn't cry. I didn't feel it. I was numb when they first told me, and I stayed numb for sixteen more years. During that time, when I would tell people that I didn't have feelings about my parents' divorce, they would invariably assure me that I *did*, in fact, have feelings and that I just didn't feel them.

That was the dumbest thing I ever heard.

Home

When I penciled my first memoir at age seven, my mom had recently married my stepfather, Mel.

My Home
My name is Margot Starbuck.
I am seven years old.
I play the piano.
I was born in Boston.

I live in Glen Ellyn Ill.

I go to school at Main Street School.

My Mother's name is Diane.

My Father's name is Mel.

My Brother's name is Scott.

My fishes name is Benji.

I like my school.

I like my relatives and all the people around me.

I love my home.

In fact, my father's name was *not* Mel. My daddy, my adoptive father Rick, had moved permanently to Connecticut the previous year when my parents had separated. Mel was my stepfather. Scott reports that I wanted to call him "Daddy Mel" immediately. Why not? The only father I'd known had just moved across the country. Nothing in my experience taught me that a parent who left wasn't lost to me forever.

Eventually I learned that my daddy would still call. He'd visit me when he was in town for business. Scott and I would get to fly on big airplanes at Christmas to visit him. All of that came as a pretty big surprise. Discovering that we were still in relationship, one not dependent on daily physical presence, might have caused another child to wonder whether her first parents might not also be lurking somewhere out there on the East Coast, too. Never once did it cross my mind.

Even if I wasn't thinking about my birth parents, someone else was. One afternoon I had been playing at Kelly Corder's house, and we were ambling back toward mine. As our yellow door came into view she asked, "What does it feel like to be adopted?" Seven-year-olds cut straight to the chase.

Without missing a beat, I assured her, "I feel special because I was *chosen.*" Even as I said it I felt a little sorry for her. When she'd been squeezed out, her parents didn't have a choice. They *had* to take her.

My mom and dad had always told me that because I was adopted I was "special." I had, after all, been chosen. Never once did I connect the dots to realize that my first mother and father had not chosen to raise me. The family story about me being chosen was a good one. It worked for me.

Though we didn't dwell on the losses involved with adoption, another girl who was close to my age, also adopted, opened a door for me to play with possibility. Her name was Annie.

I was eight when my mom first took me to see the live musical *Little Orphan Annie* at the Drury Lane Theatre in Oakbrook Terrace, Illinois. The Broadway hit is, ironically, a feel-good story about a Depression-era orphan who waits for the return of the impoverished parents who had relinquished her to the care of an orphanage. Like every other little hair-bowed, patent-leather-shoed girl wiggling in Drury Lane's plush seats, I was mesmerized by my peers on stage who looked like they were having the time of their lives. I was not, though, like every other girl in the theater.

For months after the show, at home in my pink-flowered bedroom, I played my *Annie* soundtrack cassette endlessly, belting out each word to an imaginary audience. I actually wore it out and had to beg my mom for a second copy. Although I was certainly not the first tone-deaf girl to return home from the theater bellowing show tunes, that soundtrack allowed me to voice, in a very particular way, a story I did not yet recognize as my own.

In one number, all the girls in Ms. Hannigan's orphanage pause from their grueling duties to sing "It's the Hard-Knock Life." The lively chorus that proclaims "No one cares for you a smidge" certainly bore no resemblance to my own abundance of parents. By this time I had added a stepmother to the ever-growing entourage of parental units. All of them cared for me way more than a smidge. I did not yet know that even the love of six or seven parents does not necessarily trump that of two.

In another number, the Boylan sisters' live radio commercial "You're Never Fully Dressed Without a Smile" is parroted by the girls in the orphanage. No matter what happens, the story goes, just grin and bear it. A dutiful girl, I was seldom caught without a broad, sparkly smile. If the glare did not blind others from my pain, it certainly blinded me.

Letterhead Thumbnails

It's not as if I needed more family members. My hands were pretty much full with the ones I had. With the exception of the occasional Annie induced fantasy, I gave little thought to the ghost parents who were mine. Those nameless, faceless spirits could be known only through the three slim paragraphs provided to my adoptive parents under the Boston Children's Service Association letterhead. My mother kept the precious pages tucked safely in her antique mahogany desk, along with passports, birth certificates, and the leftover stash of photos from school picture day.

Although I knew nothing about the invisible grandparents upon whom I might have unloaded a few more wallet-size photos, I always had access to the few sparse bites about my birth parents that had been provided by our Boston adoption agency. The brief report included my birth parents' nonidentifying information, which was neatly packaged as *hers, his* and *theirs.*

Her mother is in her early twenties, and of English and German nationality descent. She is 5'11" with a large build, brown hair and eyes, and a fair complexion. She has a few semesters of college and appears to be an intelligent young woman. She has recently been employed in the clerical field. Her interests are in playing the guitar, writing, and participating in sports.

My birth mother's participation in sports only fueled my growing speculation that I could be the first woman to play for the Harlem Globetrotters. Off the court, I imagined her flowing brown hair cascading over her guitar as she picked out new melodies—when she wasn't busy with her clerical duties. For a few years I thought that being employed in the clerical field meant that she was a cleric—a clergy person. So depending on the day, the rough caricature I imagined wore an athletic jersey, a Woodstock tie-dyed T-shirt or a priest's collar.

His paragraph read,

> *Her father is in his twenties, and of Dutch and Irish nationality background. He is 6'5" with a medium build, with brown hair and blue eyes, and a fair complexion. He graduated from college and is presently employed in the artistic field.*

Unfortunately, the paragraphs gave no indication of his relationship to my birth mother. I understood his biological role in procreation, but did they date? Were they engaged? Though I could visualize the shadowy silhouette of a hippy-haired mother, face tilted down toward her guitar, I could render no image of my biological father.

The few lines were all I had from which to glean a primal narrative. The final paragraph they shared was the hinge that held my disparate world together:

> *Both of her parents felt that adoption would offer the love and security they wished for her.*

She's Down!

Since I had been born on the thirteenth day of the month that also happened to be a Friday, when I was ten I began to wonder if my birth parents had been superstitious. Maybe they would have kept me if I had been born on Thursday. Who knows with these things?

In June, the week I turned eleven, we drove to Shelby, Michigan, for my first summer at Camp Miniwanca, where my adoptive parents had met. I would be away from home for five weeks. On those first few nervous nights, as we lay awake in our bunks, campers took turns telling about our families. We were all anxious to find out who had sisters and brothers and goldfish and hamsters.

My fellow campers were predictably awed by my elaborate family tree and, understandably, required occasional refreshers throughout the summer: "Now, is this your *real* mom who's coming to pick you up?" "Where does your *real* dad live?" It usually took a little conversation to figure out what each one meant by "real." The story about my many parents and grandparents rolled off my tongue like it was the greatest saga ever told. I also made sure to fill my new friends' dumb silence following the story with the quick reassurance, "There are just a lot of people who love me." If I was in a real spiritual mood, which summer camps are always good for, I sometimes even told them, "I think that God loves me *so* much that he gave me all these people who love me." Though I had no idea where my "alleged" feelings could have been hiding, my body might have offered clues.

Before breakfast each morning, all the campers gathered in front of the dining hall for some light calisthenics before reciting the Pledge of Allegiance. During that first week I was a few lines into the pledge when I fainted. Yes, I was a fainter. In kindergarten I'd gone down on the first day of my mom's new job in Chicago. That was also during the Pledge of Allegiance. Lest you question my patriotism, I can report that I also fainted the weekend I went away to Wisconsin with my friend Lori's family in fifth grade. There was neither star nor stripe in sight. No doctor ever figured out what my problem was. None ever connected the dots to reveal the outline of a brave little girl who couldn't bear being separated from her mommy. She was my anchor, the only adult caregiver who had never left me.

What's on the Outside . . .

Judging from my camp pictures, it appears as though I rarely looked in a mirror. The girls in Annie's orphanage looked like prom queens compared to what I would have seen if I'd taken the time to check. Though many of my prepubescent photos were marked with cowlicks and rats' nests, the days I *did* brush my hair resulted in six or seven braids. With a rainbow of hair bows. And the occasional jingle bell. Even the preppy garments in which my mom clothed me—monogrammed sweaters with matching corduroy pants—showed rips and stains. In fact, my parents and stepparents actually became quite concerned about my personal hygiene situation. Eventually, they worked together to develop a "Margot Improvement Program," which included an elaborate chart with stickers and rewards.

It didn't work.

My maternal grandmother, who lived in Indiana, was a card-carrying member of the Margot Improvement Program. Despite her dubious affiliation, we were very close. We could get to giggling about anything from family stories to surprisingly supportive old-lady undergarments. My grandmother taught me to paint and sew, how to roller skate and cook. When I visited her, we often said to one another that she was like my second mother.

By age twelve I had memorized her phone number. Whenever I dialed her number, my heart held the picture of her blue eyes that always shone when they saw me. She would pick up and, upon recognizing my voice, always gasp something like, "Well, hello, honey! We were *just* talking about you!" Or, "We've been thinking about you so much, sweetie. How are you doing?" She and my grandfather would then glean, with interest no less, every boring detail from my little life. I marvel now that they could sound genuinely interested in what I'd learned in babysitting class. Before we hung up, my grandmother would always assure me, "Know that we think about you *every single day.*"

No conversation concluded without some variation on the "we think about you every minute" theme. Never once did either one give me a reason to doubt it was true. It would be years before I figured out that she and my grandfather had made every one of their four grandchildren feel like the favorite I was convinced I was.

My grandparents came to visit us that fall. Every so often during this visit—and others—my grandmother would pause from sweeping out the garage or reorganizing the pantry to deliver the bits of inspirational fare she had been gathering since the last time she'd seen me. These included, but were not limited to:

- "You must brush your hair one hundred times at night, until it shines." (Like *that* was going to happen.)
- "When things don't go your way just smile and act pleasant." (That one I did take to heart.)
- "The sun is our enemy." (This was either about skin cancer, unsightly wrinkles, or some top-secret family vampire situation.)
- "If there's a feature you don't like about yourself, you must never mention it." (This one also stuck.)
- "Never slouch. Shoulders back and chest out. For good posture pretend like there's a string coming out of the top of your head that's holding you straight and tall." (The admonition was always followed by a demonstration of a brisk walk with a jaunty gait, head held high. I could almost see the marionette strings coming out of her silver helmet of hair. My cousin Joanna and I would practice it with our grandmother every summer, all three of us giggling.)
- "All the girls want to be tall like you. You're statuesque." (Not bad.)

• "If you had small feet you'd just fall over." (One of my favorites.)

During this particular visit, while nursing visions of a glorious victory at the junior high talent show, I was in the backyard working up a fabulous dance routine to Stevie Wonder's "Sir Duke." Over my black tights I wore a red and white leotard that made me feel like a mime. The subject of conversation with my grandmother had turned to my unbrushed dancer-hair. Smiling, she assured me, "God wants you to look your very best."

Very nice touch, I thought. None of my other caregivers, equally troubled by my poor grooming habits, had ever thought to invoke the divine name. It was really quite innovative.

The brazen claim, though, did not sit well with me at all. "Grandmother, how can you *say* that?" I asked, exasperated. I had always been given the impression in Sunday school that God loved me just the way I was. And this did not sound like that one bit.

"It's in the Bible," she announced, certain.

I had not read the whole Bible, but I felt fairly sure that part was not in there. I didn't know if my grandmother had read the whole thing or not. This little exchange caused me to suspect she had not. I called her bluff.

"That doesn't seem right. Where does it say that?" I demanded.

"I don't know exactly where it is, but I know it's in there," she insisted.

If it was—which I seriously doubted—I figured it must have been in the Old Testament. It did not sound one bit Jesus-y to me. Scott, a senior in high school by this time, was going to college to become a pastor. Kicking at a few fuzzy dandelions, I made a mental note to run it past him.

"Something about that just does *not* sound right. I think that God loves me just the way I am." It felt good, and sane, to say it out loud.

"Well, he *does* love you," she yielded grudgingly, "but he wants you to look the very best you can."

It was my grandparents who were responsible for my exposure to church. When I was five or six they offered Scott a quarter a week to walk me the six blocks down Pine Avenue to a local Methodist congregation. At his dollar-eyed insistence, he and I became regular churchgoers.

The mainline suburban church had a majestic, high-ceilinged sanctuary. From my vantage point, I might as well have been visiting a European cathedral. Most Sundays Scott and I would edge discreetly into one of the front pews. During the liturgical blur that preceded the children's sermon, I would crane my head to watch other children cuddled up against their parents' safe bodies.

I felt like an interloper.

I still have the Bible I received at that church as I stood beside the legitimate Sunday school kids in third grade. On that ceremonious day I listened, patiently, as a long list of students' names was read. With a last name that began with "S," I was used to waiting to hear it called. At last it was my turn: "Margot Lamar Starbuck," the teacher read. I marched dutifully across the chancel. Black leather-bound Bible in hand at last, I peeked under the cover. I must have stopped listening at the sound of "Margot," because the ornate calligraphy of my first, middle and last name took me by surprise. I couldn't figure out how anyone at the cathedral had even *known* all those names. The beautiful inscription, along with the church's name, the date and the pastor's signature had validated our covenant relationship.

I was family.

Several years later, when I was in fifth grade, a dynamic preacher was pastoring the Presbyterian church in town. When my mom and Scott began attending, I naturally fell in step. The girls in my grade at this church were called the Fizzywigs, the derivation of which can be traced back to one girl with wild red hair. Though the Fizzies welcomed me with open arms, part of me still feared rejection. This was why, despite the warm welcome, I made a special point to refer to myself publicly as an "apprentice Fizz."

Before, during and after our weekly Bible studies, we Fizzywigs would practice our dynamite dance moves. These included gyratory tracings of the letters of the alphabet. On an imaginary horizontal plane. With our hips. Along with some of the other Fizzywigs I sang in the choir, served as a youth deacon and tutored children in Lawndale, the Chicago neighborhood that was the birthplace of the Christian Community Development Association.

However, the earliest record of my spiritual journey is marked by a photo of Scott and me leaving for church when I was six or seven. Wearing a frilly smocked church dress, I'm grinning broadly and standing in front of our yellow door. Scott, behind me, wears a buttoned shirt with groovy, thick vertical stripes.

My grandmother would have been pleased. By her reckoning, *God* would have been pleased. It wasn't until years later, seeing a movie set in the Depression-torn Midwest, that I would come to understand why it had meant so much to someone from her generation to look one's very best. All I knew as a child was that my grandmother loved me. Because that counts for a lot in my book, I was more than willing to overlook a heresy so blatant it could be sniffed out by someone barely into double digits.

OK as Is

When I was fifteen years old, I flew to Connecticut to spend the summer with my dad. In the decade since we'd shared a roof, my dad had gotten remarried, had a daughter and divorced. That summer I was able to enjoy some sweet days with my five-year-old sister, Kristen. When my dad and I would pick her up at day camp or drop her off at dance class, though, I wished that the father we shared was in the state where *I* lived. I envied her that.

Although I had arrived in white pleated shorts and a red Izod shirt and carried a matching Bermuda bag, I quickly figured out that policing my wardrobe was not at the top of my dad's priority list. The sudden freedom to dress however I pleased was intoxicating. Unfortunately, with a suitcase full of clothes I'd packed from home, the only things I had to work with were the low-budget accessories I could purchase at the mall or win at the fair.

My feeble attempts to look like Madonna (and I don't mean the Virgin Mother) involved pulling my kinky-when-braided-wet-hair back with a black mesh scarf and wearing a chunky, buckled belt around my white shorts. My fingernails and toenails were usually painted in ten rainbow colors and covered in a sparkly silver glaze. The dutiful big sister, I kept Kristen's toenails looking pretty fantastic too. Although I'd been unable to wrangle one out of my mom at home, my dad provided the requisite parental signature for me to get my ear double-pierced. When I noticed that the woman piercing my ear had six or seven studs climbing her own right ear, I dared to dream of more. But first I'd let my mom get used to the second one.

One weekend my dad and I drove down to Virginia to visit his brother George's family. On our trip back north we made a point of stopping in Princeton, New Jersey, to sneak a peek at the seminary campus there. Scott, having just graduated from college, would be enrolled at Princeton Seminary in the fall.

Seminary: it sounded to me like a place where brown-cloaked monks walked around barefoot, thinking reverent thoughts. The fact that the out-of-session campus was desolate did nothing to persuade me otherwise. Although Scott didn't strike me as the monkish type, he had developed a love for scholarship in college. The quiet, I reasoned, would at least be good for that. Never once during our visit did I entertain the absurd possibility that my own glittery toes might one day call those very sidewalks home.

I had a great summer with my dad. He wasn't the man with whom I'd lived when I was young. I suppose that's always true of someone over time, but it was particularly evident in his case. During my teen years, my father had entered recovery through Alcoholics Anonymous. He had also returned to school in order to become a marriage and family counselor, and part of that training would spill over into his relationship with me. Even when we were separated by half a country, he would tell me over the phone that it just didn't matter what other people thought of me. The only opinion that mattered, he assured me, was mine. That summer he walked the talk. I could see in his eyes that I was acceptable just as I was.

Children Learn What They Live

Back at home later that summer, I recognized that things were becoming increasingly difficult between my mom and my stepfather, who also drank too much. I had lived alone with them since Scott had left for college four years earlier. Wary of sparking the next explosive argument, I managed by smiling and pleasing. For years, my mom had tried to make the best of hard situations, holding it all together for the sake of Scott and me. I confided in her that I thought she should file for divorce. Unlike my dad and Scott, there was now actually a man I *wanted* to leave my house.

A Jedi master in conflict avoidance, I laid low in the mornings by staying buried in the pages of the *Chicago Tribune*. Having no more interest in conflicts that were transpiring in the larger world than I did in the ones happening upstairs, I spent most of my mornings reading the comics and "Dear Abby" over my breakfast cereal. *Peanuts* and *For Better or for Worse* were must-reads. Once a year Abigail Van Buren would publish a column about long-lost kin, like birth parents and adopted children, reuniting. At the end of the piece she'd include the address of an international registry that matched up those searching for lost loved ones. Each time I came across it, I thought to myself, *I should probably cut that out.* Both my mom and dad had assured me that they'd support me if I ever wanted to look for my birth parents. Things like that, though, happened to other people—inky, typeset, Dear Abby people with clever pen names—not me. I never clipped it out.

Hanging over the breakfast table in our kitchen was the framed calligraphy poem "A Child Learns What He Lives." Frolicking children had been carefully painted by hand in its margins. Many mornings, I'd glance up from the *Tribune* and read, "If children live with criticism, they learn to condemn. If children live with hostility, they learn to fight. If children live with fear, they learn to be apprehensive . . ." You get the idea.

Gradually, I became more and more disenchanted with the trite ditty that seemed to mock me over my Cheerios. I longed for somebody in my home to heed the poem's warnings. I longed to scream out, with a *Peanuts* wide-mouthed bellow, "Am I the only one in this family who can *read?*"

Those desperate words that banged around inside my head never did escape. Instead, I just smiled. Like Annie and the girls.

Love Child

Although her voice lived on in my head, I no longer listened to my Annie cassette tapes. Consequently, in my teens, I really didn't spend much time thinking about being adopted. Annie was quickly replaced by R&B, funk and disco.

At age sixteen, I was listening to some of those oldies with my boyfriend Seth when we first heard Diana Ross and the Supremes' hit "Love Child." Released the month I had been conceived and quickly climbing the pop charts, it reached number one about the time my own birth mother would have discovered she was pregnant. In the song a young woman describes the pain and shame of being born out of wedlock and raised in poverty. Seth and I immediately decided that I, too, was somebody's love child. We thought it had a nice ring. Because the narrator's experience seemed worlds away from my own, however, Seth and I fancied ourselves quite funny by calling it "*my* song." After all, I'd been raised with plenty: plenty of parents, plenty of money, plenty of clothes, plenty of opportunities. I was nothing like the unwanted child in Ross's ballad.

I was *chosen*.

Not only was I different from the struggling young woman Ross describes, I was also different from so many others who are emotionally crippled by life's losses. Being relinquished by the parents who had borne me had left me completely unscathed because I had two—and then three, and four, then three again, and eventually the original two— parents who loved me. I had not been affected by living in a home with domestic violence because I had never *personally* been physically hurt. I hadn't *really* experienced my adoptive father's alcoholism because I'd been so young when we shared a home and because my mom had sheltered me from it. I certainly wasn't like those kids who are scarred by their parents' divorce, either, because my own parents had behaved so civilly. I was not affected by my mother's divorce from my stepfather that year because, after all, it wasn't like he was my *real* dad.

That I decided I was nothing like one cultural icon from the 1960s, however, in no way stopped me from fantasizing about emulating another. During my junior year of high school I joined the school's forensics team, and being seen and heard and known proved deeply satisfying. At sixteen, I began imagining that I might very well become the next Rev. Dr. Martin

Luther King Jr., and saw myself standing on a soapbox spouting fervent rhetoric about justice, freedom and inalienable human rights. I suspect that the holy convergence of the public speaking and the tutoring in that Chicago neighborhood, which was my first personal exposure to poverty, must surely have contributed to my delusion. (If I had my druthers, of course, I would have preferred to skip the "Dr." part. This sixteen-year-old was not up for a dozen more years of school.)

The fact that my amateur forensics performance of a scene from *Arsenic and Old Lace* never once took first place in a local high school forensics competition did nothing to dissuade me from the grandiose dream. Nor, apparently, did the fact that I was an over-advantaged white girl from the suburbs. That I could not reconcile my painfully unqualified demographic profile with the type of eloquent activist who might truly follow in the footsteps of the late Dr. King did not dissuade me in the least.

I just thought I'd surprise everyone.

Decisions, Decisions

As a junior in high school I began to consider attending a Christian college. I'd been impressed by Scott's experience at the one he had attended, but I did not—I repeat, did *not*—want to look like I was following in his footsteps. This ruled out his alma mater, Whitworth College, in Spokane, Washington. Thankfully, there were other interesting Christian schools.

The winter of my sixteenth year had been icy cold in Chicago, as so many of them are. That winter I received a brochure from a school called Westmont College in Santa Barbara, California. Clever recruiting strategy, I mused, with the subzero Midwest temperatures and all. It was enough to make Christians out of chilly pagans. One evening, a family in nearby Wheaton, whose sons attended Westmont, hosted an informational meeting in their home. The admissions director would be there to field questions after showing the promotional video. As we drove to the event, skidding along icy streets, my mother wanted to make sure I didn't get my hopes up too high.

"Now honey, this may be a nice video," she cautioned, "but that doesn't mean you're going to this school."

"Sure, I know," I agreed. Sort of.

I truly had the best intentions about being level-headed when it came to choosing a college. When I saw the beach in that video, though, it was all over. I thought to myself, "Oh yeah, as a matter of fact, I *am* going to this school."

California seemed like the perfect place for me since, at seventeen, I looked like the strange offspring of Pippi Longstocking and G.I. Joe. Blonde spiky hair, candy-cane striped tights, mismatched socks, rhinestone jewelry and daisy-painted combat boots did not a mother's dream (nor a grandmother's) make. When I look at the short stack of pictures I have from the period, I am forced to admit that I cannot distinguish from my clothing a typical school day from our high school's annual Wacky Tacky Day. Could we really have celebrated it five days a week?

For my school's annual Senior Ditch Day, some of the Fizzies and I made plans to go into Chicago. They no doubt were interested in hitting department stores like Marshall Fields and Carson Pirie Scott. Though I'd rather have flossed with barbed wire than shop for tasteful clothes, I was happy enough to go along for the ride. And eat lunch at Burger King.

"Mom, when we go to Chicago tomorrow can I get a third hole pierced in my ear?" I asked very sweetly.

"No."

"Please? Please-please-please-please-please-please-please?"

"No."

"Work with me. What if I get a nice outfit?" I bargained. That's when I knew I had her attention. Clothing me was her love language. Although I was not fluent, I spoke just enough to get by. Taken off guard, she paused for just a moment to strategize.

"Okay, listen," my mother reasoned like a trained hostage negotiator. "I'll give you my credit card. If you get *three* nice outfits at Marshall Fields, you can get your ear pierced."

As you might expect, most of my friends wanted my mom to be their mom.

California Girl

Before my mother and I flew out to California to visit Westmont College, my grandmother cautioned me not to talk to any flower children in California. She had no idea that I had plans to revive the movement and *be* a flower child. Right after I learned how to surf.

The school was all I'd hoped it would be. The lush campus, blooming with exotic flowers, was a short bike ride from the beach. All the students we met were friendly. I suppose there might have been classes happening, too, but I can't say for sure.

Most of the girls my mother and I passed on campus wore trendy hairstyles, fashionable outfits and cute sandals. I knew this would work in my favor with my mom; for some reason the manageable beach commute wasn't quite enough to convince her that this was the place for me. I suppose she wanted me to get a good education, but I was certain that all the tastefully dressed girls weren't hurting any.

Turning toward her beloved daughter with half-shaved head, cut-off overalls and high-top tennis shoes, my mom asked hopefully, "So honey, do you think we should go shopping for some new clothes for you?"

"No. But thanks for checking."

Mine had to have been the only family in the Midwest to hope that the child they were sending off to college in southern California might actually be *domesticated* by the experience. My family would, of course, be sorely disappointed.

I *would* be changed there, but not in a way I ever would have expected.

- two -

DUMPSTER DIVING AND
OTHER SOCIAL DISASTERS

It is my pleasure to report that the community at Westmont College warmly embraced me for who I was, eyesore packaging and all. Not only this, but I learned from my stylish new friends which hair care products would make my do even spikier. Who could have seen that coming?

I immediately noticed peers who were living differently because of their Christian convictions—and I don't just mean the boys who threw their secular cassette tapes into dorm dumpsters and the girls who refused to wear skimpy bikinis at the beach. The Westmont students who caught my attention were admittedly, in some of those ways, distinct. What was so compelling, though, were the ways in which they were also deeply *engaged* with the world. Students were involved in ministry to Santa Barbara's homeless population. They spent school breaks working alongside churches in Ensenada, Mexico. Students led summer trips to South Africa, which was at that time divided by apartheid, and helped to build bridges between white South African college students and black

Christians. I was intrigued by what I saw.

A girl named Kelly lived about six doors down from me in my first-year dorm, Page Hall. Kelly was from Arizona. She and her friend Ginger had chosen the school together and were roommates that year. That struck me as odd. Making a big life decision based on a *relationship* seemed like it bordered on irresponsible.

Both Ginger and Kelly had grown up in Christian families. Their mothers and fathers were, as they were, active in their churches. I listened attentively when Kelly talked about her father. What was most intriguing to me, besides her evident love and respect for him, was what *moved* him. More than wanting her to succeed in school or land a good job, Kelly's father wanted her to be a person who placed her trust in Jesus Christ. *How unusual,* I thought. It was an ordering of priorities with which I was unfamiliar.

Kelly was reading a book by Charles Swindoll called *Improving Your Serve.* For weeks, every time I saw it I asked her if it was about tennis. It never was. The third time I asked her if she was a big tennis player, Kelly patiently explained to me that the book was about being a servant of Jesus Christ. Kelly looked me in the eye and explained to me that the most important thing in her life was knowing and loving Jesus Christ.

As she said the words, my heart leaped within me. I had not realized, until that moment, that what Kelly had articulated was a reality. As a devoted Sunday school class member, as well as an accomplished cartoonist, I could diagram blindfolded both the sin chasm and the Jesus bridge. The reality of an ongoing redemptive relationship with God, however, had not yet sunk in. When I wondered for a moment if my high school youth group leaders and Young Life leaders had known about the whole "relationship" thing, I quickly decided that they probably did.

Now, as Kelly spoke, I suddenly felt a deep yearning to fulfill the longing I never knew I had. I was hungry for a reliable relationship in which I would be seen, heard and known. And here was a trustworthy *man* who, by Kelly's account, wanted to be in relationship with me. That part seemed almost too good to be true.

I decided that semester that knowing and loving Jesus Christ would become the hallmark of my own life as it was for Kelly's. About that time, I read somewhere that a person's relationship with God would most likely bear the marks of his or her relationship with a human father. While I could see how that might be true for many people, it was clearly not so for me. My birth parents' decision to give me up for adoption and then three divorces (my parents' and their subsequent spouses) had not put a damper on my relationship to a heavenly Father. I was, after all, special; the usual rules did not apply to me. My new relationship with a loving God, yet one more parent who loved me, only confirmed that fact.

Going Amish

Walking by the campus library one day, I passed a friend who was a premed student. As we walked by each other, Samantha broke into a huge grin and said, "Margot, you always make me so happy when I see you." I could only guess that she was referring to my groovilicious clothing, orange high-tops, matching accessories and whatever word I had shaved in the back of my head that day. I knew her kind greeting was intended to be a compliment, but it had the aftertaste of a not-compliment.

Later, as I mulled over her words, I felt a little disturbed. I began to suspect that the thing that I was known for on campus was my zany fashion sense. Never one to shy away from attention, I didn't mind being recognized; I did not, however, want to be known *only* for being a fabulous dresser. I had much loftier aspirations for my life, like eradicating injustice.

That's when I decided to go Amish.

Somehow I had gotten it in my head that the Amish, wearing plain garments to avoid attracting undue attention, had it right. To eliminate the distraction of bling, like modern zippers and shiny buttons, I planned to remove all the ear cuffs and toe rings from my jewelry box. Somehow it made sense in my jazzy, decorated little head. Although I did not go as far as wearing a cape dress and a covering, I started to mix and match boring, solid-colored clothes in my otherwise exotic wardrobe.

A week or two into the experiment, a custodian friend at the campus art center took one look at the plain version of me and asked me what was wrong. That, in itself, made me feel known and loved. Because Rob was a man of wisdom and integrity, I decided to confide in him my great plan. Since I'd only ever seen him in the modest uniform he wore to work, I assumed I would have his unflagging support.

I was shocked when he told me that he didn't see things the way I did. "Margot," he explained patiently, as if interpreting quantum mechanics for a monkey, "it doesn't matter what you wear. People will know who you are by the way you live."

Ahhhhhhhhhh. I could breathe again.

It did not take any more convincing for me to lose the simple garb.

As my dad had done in high school, a man had once again relieved me of a deep suspicion of my unworthiness by assuring me that I was acceptable just as I was. This time, I vowed, the lesson would stick.

For a moment, anyway.

B-O-B

As the second semester of school began, I attended a home basketball game with Ginger, Kelly and some other friends to cheer on our friend Nolan, who played on the team. Glancing just above whatever was happening on the court I glimpsed a man who appeared to be a new student entering the gymnasium. That moment short-circuited my entire neural network.

Charismatic, the blonde Adonis greeted the ticket-taker at the door with a hug and then pushed through the crowd as he climbed the tightly packed bleachers. Transfixed, I watched closely as he high-fived, greeted and waved to an inordinate number of people who had turned from the action on the court to beam at him. Was he a movie star? a rock icon? I squinted and strained to see if I would recognize him as someone I'd seen on MTV.

I didn't.

From my vantage point, it looked as though a royal prince was returning home after a long, brave voyage at sea. The adoring multitudes seemed to have assembled for no other reason than to hail his entry into my world. To confirm it, his loyal subjects reveled in his return with wild cheering and clapping. Because I knew that he hadn't been on our small campus the previous semester, I reasoned that he was coming back, if not from an arduous sea voyage, from *somewhere*.

Later, upon investigation, I discovered that he had returned from an off-campus program to complete a final semester before graduation. He was an art student, like me. He was a person of faith, like me. He was concerned with social justice. Me, me, me!

His name was Bob. Trembling to speak it, though, I could only choke out the alphabetic indicator, B-O-B. Nothing about *that* bodes well for an intimate personal relationship.

To make matters worse, it turned out that he was also a weird sort of school mascot. At all the subsequent home games, B-O-B would run around the court during halftime in a cheerleading skirt with a buddy— wearing a sliced-open basketball on his head—while shouting inane cheers and doing cartwheels. I have always had a weakness for guys wearing women's clothing who make fools of themselves in front of an

audience. Occasionally the pair would run across the court waving plac-
ards citing biblical references, such as ones prohibiting sexual relations
with animals. One evening, in lieu of the typical inspirational fare, B-O-B
ran across the court with one that read, "We need a date! Extension
298!"

It seemed kind of like a sign from God.

Later than evening, Ginger took it on herself to call B-O-B on my
behalf. He answered, and our conversation actually went fairly well.
Then, before we hung up, he dropped the bomb. "When you see me on
campus, introduce yourself," he suggested innocently.

To which I numbly babbled, "Oh. I don't know . . ."

I just didn't see *that* going so well. The nine earrings, spiky hair,
miniskirt and combat boots didn't exactly scream "Dream Girl." Even if
I had wanted to—and I didn't—I couldn't pull off the cute, perky, flirty
girl thing. Though meeting him was the stuff of my dreams, I was unconvinced that I would be the stuff of his. I snuck a quick glance in the
tall mirror on the back of our thick dorm room door. What I saw would
have kept my grandmother up at night.

"I'm not sure that's for the *best*," I hedged, drawing out every word as
if I'd given each one a lot of thought.

"Just say hi," he suggested kindly, as one might do with someone who
is certifiably socially incompetent.

"Yeah, we'll see. Bye."

Having been promised a girl who totally dug him, B-O-B must have
hung up feeling more than a little confused.

Dumpster Day

The next day I found myself in the school bookstore's dumpster. I truly
wish I could say this was unusual or out of character.

I had been walking past the campus store trash zone when I caught sight of some colorful envelopes beneath the container's raised and bulging lid. Upon closer inspection, I realized that an array of perfectly good greeting cards had all been thrown out. I could only assume there must be a legally binding expiration date mandating the disposal of perfectly good cards in order to avoid some dangerous bacterial infection involved with licking.

I couldn't help but think of B-O-B. My wheels started turning. Now knee-deep in garbage, I reasoned, "*He* has a sense of humor, and *I* have a sense of humor . . ."

In a hormone-induced stupor, no doubt triggered by expired envelope glue, I decided that sending him a playful series of twenty-five greeting cards through campus mail was a great idea. I know now that I should have gotten a second opinion.

Communicating with him again without our eyes having to meet probably didn't hurt either. I hadn't completely thought through how we might navigate a real relationship in the event that he was impressed and moved by "Congratulations on Your Second Child," or "Heard You Were Ill."

As soon as I dropped those cards into campus mail, any remote chance of developing a socially appropriate relationship had, albeit quite creatively, been dashed. By sabotaging that little seed of friendship with my doomed card-bundle grenade, I had preempted the rejection I knew was coming. The emotional immaturity borne from my deepest hurt did have its own canny savvy. I had made sure that, as with my birth father, adoptive father and stepfather, I *would* be left.

In the end, it didn't matter so much that he was attractive, or an artist, or passionate about justice. When B-O-B had walked into that gymnasium, it was all he had to do. The moment he greeted an old friend taking tickets at the door, he was the thing for which my heart most longed.

He was a man who came back.

Looking for Love in All the Wrong Faces

When things did not work out with B-O-B, my mind drifted back to S-E-T-H. On a cross-country road trip, I happened to be driving through my hometown while he was visiting his parents' home there. My mother had moved to southern California with her new husband the week I began college at Westmont, so on this trip I arranged to stay overnight at Seth's parents' house. Though fate had dealt me just one short evening to re-kindle romance, I was confident that I could pull it off. I dared to dream that my recently renewed affection for him would be reciprocated.

We enjoyed a delicious dinner together at a quaint little Italian res-taurant, laughing and chatting over candlelight. Although he did not verbally express his affection for me, the evening went perfectly. As I drifted off to sleep, planning the future we would share, I was certain that thoughts of me were also dancing around in his sleepy head in the next bedroom.

Early the next morning, bundled in a thick wool sweater, I braved the Midwest's winter chill to haul a laundry basket piled high with clean clothes to my car. Stepping lightly across the thick sheet of ice covering the driveway, I pushed the basket into the passenger's seat and slid in next to it in the driver's seat. Turning on the engine, I cranked the de-froster to full throttle just as my beloved appeared in the kitchen window.

Like Snow White from her own glassy tomb, I gazed into the counte-nance of my Prince Charming. The very fact that he had woken up, de-scended a full flight of stairs and looked out the window confirmed, in my mind, his undying love for me. Obviously. (The fact that I had slammed all the doors as I traipsed in and out of the house packing my car couldn't have hurt either.)

Confirming my deep suspicions, he pointed to his heart, then back toward mine, mouthing the words, "I love you."

I was giddy. Although I won't say I was surprised, given the chemistry between us the previous evening, I was nonetheless delighted. The fact that we had not kissed the night before only signaled to me that our budding long-distance romance was being built of the stuff that endures.

Coyly, I pointed to myself then back to him, echoing, "I love you, too."

From the kitchen, motioning again through the panes between us, he mouthed, "I love you."

Grinning, I returned the gesture, enjoying our flirtatious ritual.

Gradually, his motions became more insistent. Now pounding his chest with his finger, and tapping his finger back in my direction, he repeated, "I *love* you!"

Playing along, I ramped up my performance as well. Pointing to my glasses, I shouted, "*Eye!*" Then in a dramatically oversized gesticulation, which I know now should only be used by nursery school teachers, I crossed my fists across my heart and bellowed, "*Love!*" Pointing back in the direction of my future groom I hollered, "*You!*" Then, to punctuate the odd mating ritual, I thrust both arms toward the windshield with my fingers posed in the peace sign and shouted, "*Two!*" "*I love you, too!*" I hollered from the car, repeating each grand gesture.

What was *weird* was that my man would not let up. I couldn't actually hear him, but I watched as he continued to gesture frantically. Understandably, it was so hard for him to let go. Torn, yet determined, I glanced down toward the gearshift to put the car into reverse for my dramatic, heart-wrenching exit.

As I did, a bit of color caught my eye.

Glancing down, I happened to notice that a green shoulder pad from my laundry basket had become velcroed to the front of my wool sweater.

In that instant I realized that the object of my affection was, in fact, not shouting, "I love you!" Instead, in a vain attempt to get me to see the ridiculous pad stuck to my sweater, he had been pointing from his chest to mine barking, "*You have a green thing on your chest! You have a green thing on your chest!*"

Always the lady, I smiled graciously, removed the shoulder pad and pulled out of the driveway. Always the gentleman, he never mentioned it again.

It was at that point that I should have realized that my desperate longing was making me a little loopy.

Chosen and Special

Despite all the plentiful evidence to the contrary, I was convinced I wasn't one of those girls who gets caught up in trying to get a boyfriend. Not only was I adamantly *not* one of those, but I pitied—and subsequently purposed to liberate—those who were. While friends and I lounged around the dorm on Friday nights, I delivered impassioned speeches about not sacrificing yourself and your friends and your future and your faith for some dumb guy. Some of those lectures could have won an inspirational oratory competition. But I probably should have saved my breath, since the girls for whom my heart ached were out on dates with dumb guys. And some good ones.

One of those friends was Jeanie. The first week of school she had announced that she'd come to college to earn her MRS degree. It was, to be sure, a costly way to find a mate. Toward the beginning of the semester Jeanie also shared with our group of friends that her father was an alcoholic. Sad, huh? I told her I could relate, even though in many ways I could not. My mother had shielded me from my father's drinking. She had closed doors to keep me from hearing the arguing, and she had protected me from knowing he hurt her.

I have only one recollection of conflict between them; it happened when I was five years old. I had been tucked into bed and had been fast asleep when I awoke to the sound of my mother's screams. Had a trespasser forced his way into the security of our suburban home? If my mother was being attacked by an invader, why wouldn't my daddy have called the police?

My gut told me that my father and mother were not being held at gunpoint, but that something else was going on—something just as frightening. Had I been given the choice, I would have preferred the wild-eyed intruder. Lying still under pink sheets, terrified, I feared that I would be next.

Not only was I *not* next, but in the morning all four of us got up, pretended like nothing had happened, packed the car and drove off to my grandparents' home in Indiana for a merry family Christmas. A few months later my dad left for the job in Connecticut. The part of me that had felt abandoned at birth feared I would not survive if he left our home; the part born that one terrible night suspected I might not survive if he stayed. Denying both, I kept smiling. I was, after all, now loved by parents in *two* time zones.

Jeanie had seen a sign on campus for a support group for children of alcoholics. She asked me if I wanted to go. I didn't. Jeanie admitted that she was ambivalent about attending. Since I was such a great friend, I recognized how beneficial the opportunity could be for her. In a selfless gesture, I offered to accompany her to the meetings as a support friend.

Besides Jeanie and me, there were four other students in the group. Each had grown up in a home with an alcoholic parent. At each session they opened up. They spilled their guts. Tears were shed. Attentive, silent and supportive, I listened.

This went on for a good bit of the school year. I guess everyone got it

all out by April, because as the school year drew to a close, ten student
eyes and two professional ones turned on me. "Why haven't *you* said
anything?" the lips that went with the eyes demanded.

I did not like their tone one bit. They wanted to know why I hadn't
shared anything about my own situation. What was I hiding? Perhaps
they thought I was a mole, some narc from a healthy, functional family
who'd been planted to spy on them. Though I wasn't a spy, of course, I
was still a little put off by the insinuation that I might be in the same
boat with all of them. Look at them, after all—they were *crying*. You
didn't see me crying. I didn't hurt inside like they did. Sure, on the first
night I had 'fessed up to having an alcoholic parent and stepparent.
But it's not like I still *lived* with them. I was in college! See? No prob-
lems. The way I had survived my childhood home was by denying
conflict. If I didn't face it, I wouldn't have to deal with it. The strategy
had worked well.

"I came here to support Jeanie," I patiently explained. I truly believed
it. Still, it was like lying before the parole board. That, of course, bought
me an extended sentence in individual therapy.

I went one time. After detailing my complicated, eighteen-year-long
story, the shrink asked me if I felt rejected. Of all the cockamamie ideas!
Sure, my birth parents had given me up. My dad had left and moved to
the East Coast. Then the brother I trusted had left me and went to college on the West Coast. Then my stepfather had left. Rejected? Where do
they even come up with this stuff? Of course I didn't feel rejected.
Couldn't she see that I was chosen? *And* special.

Don't worry, I told her.

Road Trip

I was far more interested in the plight and liberation of oppressed peo-
ples than I was in my own emotional redemption. Occasionally Scott

would remind me that I probably had some stuff from childhood to work through. Yeah, whatever.

By fate of birth I'd missed my own country's civil rights movement, and I was not about to miss another one. During my sophomore year I prepared, with fifteen others from Westmont, for a student-led mission trip to South Africa. It was an incredible experience. Though several of us wanted to stay and continue to work for change there, our host reminded us that our own country had deep wounds that still stood in need of healing. I left inspired to go home and make a difference in the land of the free.

Back on campus, the women from our team continued to meet together to support one another in our commitment to live out a life of justice in southern California. We called our gathering a Fellowship Accountability Bible Study: that's right, FABS. Going to FABS always made me feel a little bit like a Supreme or a Marvelette.

At one of our gatherings I overheard a few of these new friends, Terry, Geni and Jane, discussing a little seed of a plan. They were chatting about taking a road trip the following summer from southern California to Vancouver. It sounded spectacular. Hesitant, I asked if I could join in.

"Of course, you nut! That would be awesome!" they assured me.

Though I heard the words with my ears, my insides found the friendly welcome as hard to believe as the one I had received years earlier from the Fizzywigs. What I had come to expect, somewhere deep in my bones, was rejection. Thankfully the rest of me accepted their gracious invitation.

When I imagined the trip in my mind's eye, I pictured a series of bohemian interstate adventures involving CB-wielding truck drivers, colorful vagabonds and the occasional carnie. The most bohemian it ever got, though, was playing charades on top of picnic tables in Vancouver with a really nice Canadian guy named Frazier. What actually happened was that, more often than not, we slept on guest beds in the homes of friends and family sprinkled up and down the West Coast. We even stopped at my mom's home outside of Los Angeles, where she now lived with her new husband, Don. Their gracious hospitality did not disappoint.

The irony of our self-indulgent journey was not lost on Terry, Geni, Jane or me. While the friends we had met the previous summer in South Africa continued to wage a valiant battle against apartheid, fighting the daily twin evils of lead foot and bed-head did pale in comparison. Our most wild evening was when Terry cut Geni's strawberry blonde hair too short and I highlighted it so that she would look cute when she returned home to her boyfriend. Graciously, though, God was faithful to meet four pilgrims seeking his face somewhere on Route 5 between Eugene and Portland. In Jane's 1986 blue Chevy Nova, something just slightly less world-changing than a national political revolution was being sewn among us.

It began brewing one night when the four of us were cuddled up in our sleeping bags in an orange pop-top VW camper van that was parked in the driveway of Terry's aunt in Tacoma, Washington. We had propped the top open so that we could drink in the night's twinkly black sky. I've always been a firm believer that there is something absolutely magical about late-night conversations between friends under starry skies. Never once have I been disappointed by one. Remembering the miniature Barbie camper vans of her childhood, Terry mused aloud, "I feel like a big hand is going to reach in and grab us." I anchored my feet under the rear seat just in case.

That night the four of us began to dream of creating a life together in Christian community once we all graduated. We would live in an urban area shoulder to shoulder with the world's poor. Some of us would enter the workforce to earn money to support the household. Others would extend hospitality to the random guests who we would welcome into our home. We expected that these guests might include unwed pregnant mothers, lonely elderly folks or people who were homeless. We decided to call the experiment in discipleship "Random House."

If my childhood home had been marked by separation, my adult one would be marked by gathering. Earnestly we prayed, "God, you know who you want us to love. Send 'em, Lord. Send 'em."

It would be the year that I learned the all-important "Be careful what you pray for" lesson.

Let's Party

At the conclusion of our road trip, I traveled east to work with an urban ministry called the Evangelical Association for the Promotion of Education, which was located in Camden, New Jersey. Everyone knew it had too many syllables, but anything better had yet to turn up.

During the six months that I was in Camden, my friends from the South Africa trip—Geni, Terry and Jane—became friends with Kelly, my friend who had lived down the hall and talked with me about her relationship with Christ. When I returned, the five of us shared a house together. It was my final semester of college. Terry and I scored our own rooms, while Geni, Jane and Kelly shared a room with one large futon. They were tiny people. Geni was still dating, but *no one* was bringing anyone home to share either the crowded bedroom or the spacious ones.

The previous year I had served in the dorms as a resident assistant, and this year I decided to organize a little reunion in our cool house for the girls who had lived in my hall. The only official replies I received to my party invitations were some "I'm so sorry I can't make it" responses and a handful of "I have plans but I'll try to stop by."

Having kicked my housemates out for the evening, I waited alone in front of a half-dozen carefully prepared hors d'oeuvre platters. I stretched out on the couch, crunched a few carrots and ate some cookies. For the first twenty minutes or so I was able to convince myself that all my guests were being fashionably late for a party scheduled to start at eight.

At half past eight, I started to worry. I began piecing together the worst possible social scenario. Ironically, the horror evolving in my imagination never involved *no* guests. If no one showed up, I would still have been able to convince myself that there was some big concurrent event of which I'd had no knowledge—no doubt some mandatory Friday night study session.

No, what I dreamed up was far worse. The most horrible prospect I could envision would be for *one* guest to show up. She would just be planning to pop in and chat for a few minutes on her way to a better party. The truth of my social tragedy would, at that point, become real to me. Having a witness would make it all the more difficult to convince myself it wasn't personal.

The thought was more than I could bear.

I quickly began concocting excuses to counter the queries of my banished housemates upon their return. They'd walk in after a fun night with friends over pancakes or frozen yogurt and ask innocently, "How was the party, Margot?"

"What *I* really want to know is how was *your* evening?! Let's hear about *that* fun stuff!" I'd answer, feigning interest in their lives.

Words spoken to another party host began to force their way into my head: "When you give a luncheon or a dinner, do not invite your friends or your brothers or your relatives or rich neighbors, in case they may invite you in return, and you would be repaid" (Luke 14:12).

Well, I reasoned, there was no chance of being repaid for the lovely evening none of my friends had enjoyed. Phew! I was off the hook—even if my party was not. Jesus continued, "But when you give a banquet, invite the poor, the crippled, the lame, and the blind. And you will be blessed, because they cannot repay you, for you will be repaid at the resurrection of the righteous" (Luke 14:13-14).

I was back on the hook.

The girls I had invited to my party had all been first-year students the previous year. Some might say these vulnerable ones qualified as poor and lame. Some might, but I wouldn't. "Okay, God, okay," I thought. "This is a really dramatic and humiliating way for you to make your point, don't you think?"

In an instant, I knew what I needed to do. There was no audible instruction from heaven, no angelic visitation; it was just a holy hunch. Pensive theological reflection soon shifted to embarrassment management. Truth was, I didn't want to be around when my housemates got home. I certainly didn't want to be around when that one lone guest poked her head in to make her pity stop. So at forty-nine minutes past the appointed hour, I furiously started packing up food and beverages. Juggling cups, plates and generic plasticware, I flattened the back seat of my red Ford Escort and started loading it up. I was like a professional burglar from one of those reality shows in which the thief is given four minutes to clear out a house. Veggies, baked goods, fruits, ice cream and drinks were all quickly stolen away.

Several minutes later, I pulled into a vacant lot across the street from the local homeless shelter. I carried a small tray of goodies in front of me like an ID swipe card. I hoped it would get me in the door.

It did.

Although no one spoke, I suspect that, had cartoon bubbles floated over the heads of those gathered around the television, they might have read "What's Martha Stewart doing here?" Reaching a dining area where a few men sat talking, I laid a platter of food on an empty table. Sensing again that I owed some explanation for my intrusion on their quietude, I spit out in one apologetic breath, "Got-food-if-you-want-some-help-yourself."

Each one politely took a small carrot stick.

Certain now that my harebrained idea had not been divinely inspired and was mine alone, I noticed a woman in her fifties, with a colorful scarf wrapped around her head, glide into the room. Thin and sprightly, she had tanned skin, leathered by the elements. Her vibrant eyes danced, seeming to belie her current lot in life.

I grunted another curt explanation-slash-invitation.

Turning, the woman started to wind her way through the facility's hallways back toward the crowded room. In an unhurried southern drawl, she called out gently throughout the facility: "Come in hither! Come and dine. Come in hither! Come and dine."

If it ever had been my party, which now seemed doubtful, it was no longer.

"Come in hither! Come and dine." The cadent welcome echoed through the building. I heard in the musical tone of the woman's voice an edge of mischievous delight. I wondered briefly where she had learned the wonderful phrase, and if she ever missed the person who had originally issued it. I think I would have.

The party's new hostess continued to weave in and out of bunk rooms and public spaces sounding out the glorious cry: "Come in hither! Come and dine."

Though the woman spoke only those six words, the fullness of God's own invitation through the prophet Isaiah rung in every syllable. To a beloved people who had been suffering in exile God had breathed,

Ho, everyone who thirsts, come to the waters; and you that have no money, come, buy and eat! Come, buy wine and milk without money and without price. Why do you spend your money for that which is not bread, and your labor for that which does not satisfy? Listen carefully to me, and eat what is good, and delight yourselves in rich food. Incline your ear, and come to me; listen, so that you may live. (Isaiah 55:1-3)

The second nearly empty room I had been unable to fill that night soon flooded with party guests. They were still enjoying one other's company when I finally left, full.

It was entirely evident to me that those who had gathered in the homeless shelter's kitchen that night were entirely embraced in the heart of God. In fact, I was more certain of God's love for them than of his love for me.

And there's the rub. I had become convinced that God cared for the poor, the marginalized and the needy. He loved the ones sleeping on bunk beds in shelters in Santa Barbara and the ones infected with HIV in South Africa. I knew—no questions asked—that these ones, made in God's own image, were *worthy* of God's attention, nurture and provision.

Me, though? I just didn't know.

A pushy new housemate would soon force me to entertain that very question, the one that I had been working so hard to avoid.

- three -

LOVE CHILD

One evening in April, Geni gathered us together for a house meeting. She didn't say what was on the agenda. My first thought was that it would be related to the dirty dishes I had left in the sink or the bacteria-infested cup that I always kept on the windowsill for easy access. (I had, to my credit, marked it in acrylic paint with a skull and crossbones to give any thirsty visitor fair warning.)

Geni's expression was somber as she led us into the large bedroom. We all stretched out on the futon, arms and legs draped over one another, and waited to hear whatever it was we needed to work through together. I silently hoped the ax would fall in someone else's direction.

Finally, Geni choked out the reason she had called us together: she was pregnant. Her relationship with her boyfriend had been more serious than any of us had realized. Stunned, the five of us struggled to process what Geni had shared and what it would mean for her future. Though I couldn't squeeze out any tears, I did join in the few needed laughs the five of us were finally able to share. The ax *had* fallen. A world of possibilities had suddenly been baby-gated off, and

Geni was the one trapped by the new boundaries.

Geni had a number of older Christian friends in town. After praying and seeking out wise counsel from these friends, she made the decision my own birth mother had not. Opting against adoption, Geni chose to raise her son.

I found myself conflicted during Geni's pregnancy. In fact, I was as voiceless as I had been twenty-one years earlier. While other friends offered their opinions about what Geni should do, I said nothing. To have lobbied for adoption would have felt like sanctioning the bumpy story that had been mine; to have lobbied for anything else felt even more threatening. Stuck, I remained silent. The survival pattern I had developed in childhood—avoiding conflict—actually kept me from caring for Geni the way I thought I should.

Geni's pregnancy was difficult. During her first trimester she was let go from her job as a bank teller. By her second trimester she and her boyfriend had broken up. During her third, Geni suffered a ruptured appendix while working the night shift at her new job. She weathered each blow by turning her face toward the Lord's for provision, intimacy and health. She received all three.

Well into Geni's eighth month, when she was still healing from the small surgical incision carved into a constantly growing midriff, she, Terry and I asked God to provide a home we could share in Santa Barbara when our "Muffin" was born. Being rejected by a series of landlords had taught us that no one wants to rent a two-bedroom apartment—which is all we could afford—to three women and a baby.

The final one to reject us was Mrs. Manilla. Yet strangely, after she had told us no, Mrs. Manilla called back several days later to say that she had changed her mind and that we could have the townhouse on Pitos Street after all. She never did say why.

During the week we were moving in, I stumbled on a brown plaque at a local thrift store. Teetering on the edge of terribly unattractive, it looked as if it had been designed for the kitchen or living room of someone who enjoyed decorating in earthy tones. I'm typically not a "plaque" person, and I wouldn't have given it a second thought any other year. The beige text proved irresistible to me, however, as the three and a half of us began our life together: "Home: Where each lives for the other and all live for God."

After paying for it, I brought it straight home and hung it in the brown kitchen of our new two-bedroom duplex.

Starstruck

I had graduated from college with no job offers and nothing more than a vague plan about sharing life with Geni, Terry and Muffin. Basically, I was every parent's worst nightmare. There were many naysayers in my extended family who doubted that I would be able to support myself. This absolutely infuriated me. I'd show them.

So I got three jobs.

In the early morning hours, I delivered bread to restaurants and grocery stores. Then I worked in a senior daycare center until noon. After that I cared for an elderly woman living in her daughter's home. On the side, I was launching what was to be the first of many failed small businesses. This one was called Starstruck Creative Clothing. I bought the most brilliantly colored dresses from thrift stores, in fabulous psychedelic patterns, so that I could cut swatches from them to sew onto the denim clothing that I dyed pink, green, purple and orange. There were also some very spectacular trims involved.

I had found the pièce de résistance that inspired it all during my first year of college at a thrift store on Santa Barbara's Milpas Street. It was an electric orange muumuu. The floor-length dress, made from a swirly orange Polynesian design, featured patches of brown and hot pink.

Though I had no ostensible reason to wear a muumuu, I couldn't just *not* purchase that gorgeous thing. It was a matter of principle. I kept it safely tucked away until the perfect opportunity to wear that awesome dress should present itself.

If you can believe it, that never happened.

After moving in with Geni and Terry, I cheerfully went about my Starstruck Creative Clothing work, gathering the garments and fabrics and trims that would launch my career in alternative fashion. Not counting the abysmal sales, carpal tunnel syndrome and the occasional carpet-buried needle through the foot, it was a very satisfying endeavor.

Kelly stopped by our home one day while I was working and noticed the familiar orange muumuu from our first weeks of college. Wryly, she noted, "And there's the fabric that just won't die."

I wouldn't allow it. It was too spectacular. I finally decided to harvest the orange fabric, gleaning quite the impressive yardage from the floor-length dress that fit someone almost six-feet tall. I stitched bright patches of it to a denim jacket and baseball cap so that I could wear them every day of my life. Which, of course, I did. When I wore that juicy orange fabric, I felt like *me*.

I had not accounted for one thing in the custom clothing business. While even the most stylish women often admired the zany carnival fashions on *me*, not everyone felt comfortable dressing as flamboyantly as I did. So while a local housewife might have been able to appreciate some of these colorful garments, she wouldn't have been caught dead wearing one.

Treasure Chest

My most dependable paycheck came from my mid-morning employment at the senior center. On a typical day we might watch a slideshow of someone's trip to Hawaii, play Bingo or listen to a well-meaning volunteer hammer away on the accordion.

One of my closest friends at the center was Ben. In the 1960s, Ben Wright, a bus driver at the time, was better known as Santa Barbara's own Honko the Clown. I had been unaware that cities had their own patron clowns until Ben mentioned it. Once I knew it was *a thing* I realized that Chicago's patron clown was probably Bozo.

Ben talked me into being his assistant for the crowning clown act of his career, which we would perform together at the center. In addition to a few magic tricks, Ben taught me how to cut out a circle of paper dolls for the show. We had never done that fun thing when I was an art major in college.

On the big day, I picked Ben up early so that we could prep for the show. When we arrived at the center, I applied his white face, and mine. Surveying my work, I was grateful his vision was going. I wanted him to be proud of his final performance. I slid into the fabulous pink and orange polka-dot costume I'd chosen from Ben's garage and helped him into his.

As we hid outside, waiting to be introduced, I whispered to Ben, "I hope we do good!"

Confidently, he assured me, "It's got to be better than the girl who played the accordion."

Though I secretly suspected Ben was using the whole "last show before I die" routine to get a young woman into his living room, I didn't mind. If I lived alone at eighty, I'd want a young woman in my living room too.

I loved it that Ben had chosen me to be his lovely assistant and invested his time into making me a great one. I loved it that every day gracious Phoebe noticed and admired my twenty-two-year-old teeth. I loved it that Minnie and I sang songs together like "What a Friend We Have in Joe" and "Joe Is So Good" while we waited for her husband, Joe, to pick her up each day.

I loved being around that wonderful crowd because I did not expect any one of them to reject me.

Out of the Oven

I learned that year that babies are pretty good for that too. This I had not known.

In an attempt to prepare me for life after Muffin arrived, well-meaning friends and relatives warned me how stressful it can be to live with an infant. Was I prepared, they demanded, for the horrible sounds and smells and responsibilities which were coming my way? Confessing I was not, I braced for the worst.

Each one of us in the home had special jobs to do around Muffin's birth. Geni, of course, had to squeeze the kid out. That seemed like plenty. Terry read all the birthing books and attended the Lamaze classes with Geni. She was the capable, well-read birthing partner. Not being a big fan of oozy placentas or cracked nipples myself, I was Geni's *other* personal assistant. As her due date approached, I frosted her hair so that it would look good in those first pictures with Muffin. I was also slated to drive to the hospital and, once there, to videotape the birth.

A few hours after we had all gone to bed on October 22, Geni flipped on the light in the room Terry and I shared, waking us to let us know that her water had broken. Though normally difficult to rouse, Terry was up in a flash and had taken charge.

"Margot, you put her bag in the car," Terry instructed. "I'll help Geni get ready."

I loaded up the trunk and rolled a few feet down the driveway so the car's back door was flush with the walkway in front of our home. Terry gently guided Geni into the back seat and slid in beside her.

For months I had been looking forward to speeding on our way to the hospital. I thought doing eighty-five or ninety might be nice. I had carefully worded an elegant defense that I would offer to any police officer who dared pull us over. Once the precious cargo was actually loaded up, though, reckless driving completely lost all appeal.

Having delivered Geni and Terry safely to the emergency-room entrance, I parked and went inside. After several hours of labor, Geni delivered Isaiah James Everett at 7:49 a.m. on the morning of October 23 with camera rolling. The minidocumentary that I produced captured each moment, from Isaiah's skull crowning into view until the rest of him finally squirted out too. It was truly spectacular. Ask anyone—neighbors, mail carrier, UPS guy. We forced all of them to watch it.

To think that fifteen months earlier Geni, Terry and I had *not* been grabbed from an orange VW camper and gripped by a hand more powerful than our own began to seem more ridiculous than the increasingly evident fact that we had. God's steadfast faithfulness to Isaiah and to Geni was absolutely palpable during those days and months. God's love being lived out in our affordable quarters, each living for the other and all living for God, is what made it a *home.*

After he had been fully baked and ejected from the oven, we no longer called Isaiah "Muffin." Instead, he quickly became our sweet little Bugaboo. In the midst of all the doomsday diaper warnings, no one had thought to tell me how wonderfully fantastic Isaiah would be. That Bug was the most precious little lump of molecules I'd ever met. As I cradled that amazing little boy over the first few months of his life, staring into his wide eyes, something long-buried was released inside me. Squeezing each of his tiny fingers and toes, I found myself asking the question that, ostensibly, should have been answered in seventh-grade health class: "Where did he *come* from?"

Asking it of Isaiah called forth the deep wondering in my own heart: "Where did *I* come from?" The vault that had protected my heart from so many early serial ruptures had been cracked open by the trusting gaze of a seven-pound bundle of boy.

DNA Terrorists

Several years before, during my sophomore year of college, my dad had offered me some literature he'd received from an adopted friend about a group called the Adoptees' Liberty Movement Association, or ALMA. Somehow in his original verbal explanation I heard Adoptees' *Liberation* Movement; thus I began visualizing adoptees carrying machine guns and forcing reluctant birth parents to buy them birthday presents. Gun shy, I filed the information away with my cherished paragraphs from the adoption agency in a manila folder I kept that was marked "Adoption." I later learned that this is not the case with ALMA at all.

During college, I still hadn't thought a lot about my birth parents. With all the stepparents and ex-stepparents, there just was not a lot of disk space left on my heart's hard drive for two more.

Soon after Isaiah was born, a friend sent me an article she had clipped from the local paper. I slid it in next to the ALMA envelope.

> *Dear Abby: I am a first-time writer, and it's about time. In November, 1983, you ran a letter in the San Diego Union about the International Soundex Reunion Registry [ISRR]. It gave me the information I needed to find my birth mother. I won't ramble on about our reunion, but suffice it to say it was terrific. I met my birth mother shortly after my 24th birthday. Abby, thank you for the best birthday present I could have asked for.*
>
> *Gratefully Reunited in San Diego*

The reunion registry's address was printed in Abby's reply. What my scissors-wielding friend did not realize, of course, is that I had read a variation of the same article over my breakfast cereal every year of my life, between the time of achieving literacy and leaving for college. It was that column that did *not* apply to me.

I had, out of curiosity more than anything else, actually requested an application from the registry about the time my dad gave me the ALMA information. Now, sliding the newspaper clipping into the adoption file next to what I had on the suspected DNA terrorists, I pulled out the application from the ISRR. Scanning the page, I noted proudly that I had completed it to the best of my ability and carefully stuck it back in the manila safety zone. They say the odds of a reunion increase if the form is actually placed in a stamped, addressed envelope and sent to the registry.

Before Isaiah's earth-shattering gaze had returned mine, I had not had sufficient motivation to risk wondering about, let alone investigating, my roots. Why go looking for another parent who could reject me? Since Bug's arrival, though, I'd become more curious. As his little features began to take shape, I couldn't help but glance in the mirror and wonder where I'd gotten mine. The remote possibility that there might be a real live birth mother or a breathing father out there in the world had suddenly captured my imagination.

Though intrigued, I was still ambivalent. I was not prepared to embark on a *search,* like the ones where some poor soul featured on an evening news show hires a detective and they repeat the same blurry brief video clip over and over again. The registry, though, seemed harmless enough. If no profile could be paired with mine, they wouldn't even bother contacting me; they'd only reply if a match was made. Registering with that great big agency didn't seem like it could hurt. A search that ended in rejection could.

I pulled out the form once more. As I folded it up and slid it into the envelope provided by the agency, I soothed myself with the thought that, most likely, nothing would ever come of it. The chances seemed pretty slim, as I couldn't even identify the hospital in which I'd been born. I finally dropped that registration into the mouth of the big, blue mailbox on the corner when Isaiah was three months old. Having convinced myself that nothing would result, I would not, could not, be rejected.

Dad Says Hello

A week later, toward the end of February, I came home from work to find a phone message scrawled on the back of an envelope in Geni's handwriting.

> *Margot-*
> *Int'l Soun ____Registry? Sarah Bryant has some news for you. Please call between 9-4. Dad says hello.*

My jaw dropped. This couldn't be happening. The registry wasn't supposed to contact me unless they had news. That was, after all, the beauty of the whole plan. No rejection.

A match had been made and it was with my birth father! I had not seen that one coming. I knew that women, both birth parents and their children, were much more likely to search out lost kin than men. I'd seen other people's tall and small birth mothers on Oprah's couch, but I had no idea what a sample birth father would look like. Did they have beards? Did they wear cowboy boots? Did they sport tattoos? I felt dizzy. He had said hello to me. Who just says hello after twenty-two years? Apparently, this guy did.

I quickly decided that I would not tell my adoptive family until I knew exactly what was going on. I wanted to enjoy the freedom to be excited without worrying about hurting anyone. Although my parents had always said they would support me they were, after all, still human. I suspected it would sting.

When nine o'clock rolled around the next morning, I was already at work at the senior center, so I asked for permission to use the office phone. Thankfully my boss was a new mother; when I told her what I was doing, the entire office burst into excited tittering.

After a few rings I got through to the agency and was connected to Sarah, the worker assigned to my case. Sarah began by telling me that she had gotten my phone number from my adoptive father, in Connecticut. The trigger reminded me that, because I had not allowed myself to expect anything to come of the registration, I had not even given the current address or phone number for where I now lived with Geni, Terry and Bug. Knowing my contact information would expire in six months when I moved on, I had listed phone numbers and addresses for my mom in Santa Monica and my dad in Connecticut.

Aha! So it wasn't my birth father who had sent his greetings through the agency at all. It had been my *adoptive* dad, Rick, who had said hello. That made more sense. He said hello all the time.

Sarah confirmed that she was looking at a registration that a birth mother had submitted two years earlier, from information she'd been given when she placed her child. Sarah asked me to verify a few facts about my adoptive parents. "It says that your adoptive parents enjoyed traveling, skiing and playing tennis together," the voice from Nevada prompted.

"Umm . . ." I searched, wanting it to be them. I ventured, "I guess that sounds like them."

After stumbling through a few more questions about my adoptive parents, Sarah wanted to know what I knew about my birth. I still didn't know the name of the hospital. She asked about my birth weight.

"I know I have it on a piece of paper at home," I explained, visualizing my manila adoption folder. "I'm at work right now."

She instructed me to call her back when I could confirm the information.

My boss, now fully enmeshed in my little soap opera, sent me straight home to get the information. No one else was there. Bounding up the stairs to the room I shared with Terry, I thumbed through my personal records, grabbed the adoption file and ran back downstairs.

Dialing the agency from our kitchen phone, I spat out, "Eight pounds, thirteen ounces."

The voice on the other end, holding her own pair of adoption folders, confirmed it: "This is your birth mother."

Later that day Sarah arranged for my birth mother and me to speak on the phone the following morning, a Saturday. Ten o'clock would give me plenty of time to get home after my morning bread-delivery route.

Having already spoken to my birth mother, Sarah told me that her name was Pam and gave me her phone number and address. In addition to the information I already knew from Pam's letterhead paragraph, I then learned a little more when Sarah let some private information slip. It was information that my birth mother would choose not to mention when we spoke the next day.

When I was born, my name was Tama.

Happy Girl

I gave everyone in our home strict instructions not to answer the phone on Saturday morning. After my bread delivery I rushed home to wait, poised on my bed with journal and pen. The phone rang just once when I grabbed it.

"Hello?" I spit out.

"Hello, is this Margot?" came a nervous voice on the other end.

"It is. Hi." I was nervous too. I also felt just as excited and dorky as I had talking to B-O-B. Someone *had* come back, for me.

It was hard to believe I was speaking with Pam. Harder still to comprehend was that there *was* a Pam. Although she's the one that others usually meant when they asked about my "real" mom, that morning was the first time she actually seemed real.

We took turn introducing ourselves. I liked Pam's sense of humor. I blathered on about my perfect life, and Pam shared about her childhood and family in Virginia. She had lived in Massachusetts for a few years before I was born. Pam had been just my age, twenty-two, when she'd given birth to me. Subsequently she'd had no other children.

As we spoke I jotted down every detail, filling in shades of the faint line-drawn, guitar-strumming caricature with which I'd lived for so long.

Pam and my birth father, Max, had met and dated in 1968, she explained, when they both worked in Boston for the summer. Now that I was *officially* a love child of the sixties, I would affectionately come to think of it as "the summer of love." Pam and Max had been in their early twenties. Their relationship ended amicably when they parted in the fall and Max returned to his home in Illinois. Soon after they separated Pam realized that she was pregnant. Wanting more for "the baby" than she was able to give—wanting more for *me*—Pam chose to relinquish me for adoption. When she informed Max of her decision, he didn't protest. Toward the end of Pam's pregnancy Max drove back out to Boston to visit Pam in the Florence Crittenton Home, a residence for unwed mothers.

One little piece of Pam's story stuck in my craw. She told me that Max had driven out again to see her in the hospital after I had been born. When Max showed up in her hospital room, though, Pam—whose hormones were more than a little out of whack—really let him have it. She yelled at him and sent him away.

I didn't want their story to end like that. I didn't want *my* story with him to end like that. I desperately wanted to believe that, exiled from the recovery room, he had furtively made his way down the hall to the baby nursery. I wanted to imagine that he had searched frantically for the swaddled baby labeled with Pam's last name. I couldn't bear the thought of him leaving Pam's room, stepping into the elevator and hitting the star-marked lobby button. I wanted to believe that he had made a point to see me because he had so wanted to lay eyes on me.

I wanted to believe it, but deep down I didn't.

Photos

During that first phone call, Pam and I agreed to exchange pictures. Always one for a big production, I created an elaborate timeline of the last twenty-two years, including big moments like being diagnosed with lazy eye at four and playing a townswoman in my junior high school production of *Calamity Jane*. Because what birth mother wouldn't want to know that great stuff? The photo collage I created included the iconic moments from my perfect childhood. There was one of me grinning in my purple Owls baseball uniform. There I was, smiling in my green Hilltoppers basketball uniform. And there, resting in front of the yellow door, grinning in my polka-dotted clown costume on Halloween, even though I didn't yet know any cool clown tricks. It was entirely obvious from the collage I created, the one on paper matching the one I had pasted together in my mind, that I was a happy girl who'd had a *very* happy childhood. Finding Pam was simply a continuation of the "God Loves Me So Much That He Gave Me All These People Who Love Me" story.

Our pictures must have crossed in the mail somewhere around Nebraska. When Pam's arrived, I tore open the package. She had written a note on beautiful salmon stationery. It read, "This peach paper is the color you were wearing the last time I saw you. You were about three weeks old and adorable—of course."

Of course.

It wasn't hard to do the fashion math. Both of my mothers had held

me when I was wearing the orange dress that had been chosen for me by
a social worker for my big day. In it I had been both released and claimed.
In it, I had been loved and I had been loved.

The earliest picture of Pam that she included in my packet was from
the first grade. When I saw her dark brown hair and big, dark eyes I
feared, for a moment, that there might have been a mistake at the registry. I saw little resemblance to the blonde-haired, blue-eyed, freckly girl
in my own first-grade picture. Pam's brunette graduation picture from
high school was equally troubling.

Thankfully, Pam also included photographs from the summer of love.
The single picture taken of Pam and Max had been clicked when she was
just my age, twenty-two. Her summer blonde hair and familiar profile
next to his convinced me that there was no mistake. We were blood.

Pam also sent photocopies of drawings that Max had sketched of her
when he'd visited her during pregnancy. She looked a little sad. One
sketch was a close-up of her hand. He'd drawn her wearing a ring on her
wedding finger, and although it was clearly not a wedding ring, it had
his signature over it. I wasn't sure what to make of that. I secretly hoped
it meant that their union was strong enough that now, decades later, he'd
be curious about the fruit of it.

Pam also sent a cassette tape that she and Max had made while driving along in his truck. Terry was home when it arrived in the mail, and
I wanted her to listen to it with me. Together we huddled on the carpet
in front of a cassette recorder set on an old trunk in the living room.
Nervously, I pushed the play button.

"It's up to you, baby. It's your bag . . ." giggled Pam. I thought she
sounded very groovy.

Max began, "It's, uh, the end of September. My name is Max Edwards
. . . that sounds stupid. I'm Max."

Terry turned to look at me, eyes wide.

Max began to babble on about the blue sky and the green traffic light.

"Come on," Pam urged.

"Um . . ." he attempted. "The truck's running like a jewel. I really don't know what else to say."

"You start with a biography; you have to give a brief biography," she urged.

Reluctantly, he obliged. "Born in Illinois, in the year of '45. Grew up like Huck Finn, landed in high school, was a schmuck. Played a little soccer, ran track, college All-American, and became a painter."

Terry shot me another glance. Drinking in every word, neither one of us spoke.

With intermittent encouragement from Pam, and regular comments about his '51 Ford truck, Max reluctantly spit out his bio. The narrative included the name of his high school, his world history teacher, colleges, jobs.

The tape ended when he wearied of telling his life story.

Turning toward each other, Terry and I were both wide-eyed. I was wide-eyed because I was listening to a recording that had been made when I was about sixteen cells big in my mother's womb and that sounded as if it had been scripted entirely for my benefit twenty-two years later. The tape was exactly the kind of time-capsule memorabilia thing I'd made my own reluctant friends do throughout high school and college. I had never met anyone else who chronicled like me.

I didn't know why Terry was wide-eyed.

"Margot!" she exclaimed. "He sounds *just* like you!"

I really hadn't noticed. As a girl I had listened to the old family cassettes that Scott had made of two-year-old Margot. My Boston accent had made me a dead ringer for a tiny little guest hostess on NPR's auto maintenance talk show: "My name is *Mah*-got La-*Mah Stah*-buck, and welcome to *Cah Tahk!*" After we had moved to Illinois, the accent had quickly been replaced by the Midwestern twang I now shared with my birth father.

Orange Dress Day

Learning more of Pam's history, I was able to piece together more of my own. The family story told by Scott, just five years old when I was adopted, is that on the day he and my parents picked me up from the adoption agency, I had cried the entire way home. Though I wrote it off for years as the playful ribbing of a jealous sibling, I suddenly found myself speculating that his story might be true.

Pam explained that I had spent six days in the hospital with her. She had given me a name. When she spoke to me she had called me "Tama." I have no reason to doubt that when I was born I knew that Pam was mine in the same way that any other newborn knows her mother's heartbeat and temperament and the cadence of her voice. We were certainly *not* strangers.

Pam's social worker had arrived on day six to take me to a foster home. Pam reported that the woman was very kind. Two weeks later the same woman transported me to her office and put me back into Pam's arms. Pam held me, spoke my name and cried. She told me I was beautiful in my orange outfit.

Eventually Pam gave me back to the stranger.

On the same day, my adoptive parents and brother Scott arrived to take me home. They called me Margot and changed me out of my orange outfit.

Of course I cried all the way home with my new parents.

Finders, Keepers

Finding Pam was like discovering a handful of missing jigsaw puzzle pieces to a self-portrait that was slowly beginning to take shape. The newly emerging edges, though, just made me want to hunt harder for the pieces I was still missing. I knew I'd find them. My grandmother had always told me I was a great *finder*—locating her misplaced glasses case or a lost *Guideposts* magazine. I'd taken her words to heart.

It wasn't just stuff that I found: I had a knack for spotting people too. I would spot people I knew from school or church or Girl Scouts many miles from where they should be, sometimes out of state. I would see them at a Cubs' game, the zoo, or even at a rest stop on the way to Camp Miniwanca. Some were glad to be found, while others—not so much.

It's a gift, like Superman's x-ray vision. In the world of superheroes, I'm the smart-looking one with a hair bun and lime green cat-eye glasses who's called on to locate a lost toddler wedged in a well or sniff out an evil villain holed up in the New York City sewer system. Sure, I spot the usual variety of celebrities at airports, movie theaters and beaches. I won't bore you with the full list. All I'll say is this: Oliver North has to be scanned when he goes through airport security, just like the rest of us. Mindy Cohen, who played Natalie on *Facts of Life*, shops for her own produce. And Jamie Lee Curtis subscribes to actual news magazines. They're exactly the same ones you and I read. It's true.

I already knew I was a great finder. I didn't know that I was about to make the greatest find of all.

-four-

SLEUTHING AROUND

The year with Terry, Geni and Isaiah was a pensive one for me, as I reflected on my burgeoning sense of identity and made plans for the future. The day that I received the phone call about Pam from the reunion registry, I had actually written "Who am I?" at the top of the day's to-do list, right over "Buy milk" and "Get gas." That's a little ironic. And self-involved.

Toward this end of self-discovery, I kept a running list of personal theories I was testing out. I hoped that by chronicling things that I believed in, I might just be able to edit them all together into a coherent self. For example, my "Pre-trip Hype Theory" maintained that when there's too much excitement *before* a road trip, the trip itself becomes a letdown. Many of my other important theories were similar common-sense observations; for example, Geni and I developed a "Cracklin' Oat Bran Theory." It goes like this: "When you're so poor that you can't afford the big things in life, at *least* buy good cereal." It goes without saying that none of these were run through any sort of ethical orthodoxy filter before I jotted them down in my thick blue notebook.

Another theory that I developed as we shared life together was the one on being in love. In my opinion, being "in love" was a far cry from experiencing *real* love. I concluded:

> Being *"in love"* is like temporary insanity. It's an illness that doesn't have much to do with love at all. "Falling" in love is like falling into an abandoned well shaft.

I was a real treat to be around.

As life got back to normal after my first conversation with Pam, I returned to the regular concerns that had occupied my thoughts a few days earlier: breakfast cereals, dirty diapers and other people's love lives. When we had originally conceived our Random House, we'd thrown around a few ideas about guys and dating and marrying. We had never spelled out any official house policy on dating, however, or even how much time we would spend with each other that year.

So when Terry began spending a lot of time on the other side of our duplex with a boyfriend who lived there, I realized that this scenario had not been part of my fantasy about intentional community. I was concerned about this change to our lives, even though I liked her boyfriend and even though we all did fun stuff together, like playing household appliance charades and dancing to Van Morrison.

I came by my reticence honestly. I had agonized as I watched women compromise who they were in order to snag or keep a man—not necessarily even a *good* man. I knew I came off as a prude, but so much of my life had been determined by the men who had been attracted to my beautiful mother. How I wish she would have had girlfriends as uptight and judgmental as I was.

Now Terry had been swept off her feet by a guy. If I was honest, it probably wasn't even the sweeping I minded per se as much as it was the time not spent at home with Geni and Isaiah and me.

Basically, I was jealous.

The Great Thing About Hebrew

I poured out the concerns of my Grinch-like "three-sizes-too-small" heart before God. I hated feeling so mad, jealous and selfish about losing Terry to a man. As I journaled and prayed, a Scripture verse popped into my mind, the words mysteriously creeping into my frontal lobe and demanding my attention. They were something along the lines of, "If you live according to the flesh you will die." The message resonated immediately. Although the Holy Spirit was probably talking about me, I immediately thought of Terry.

I flipped open the NRSV Bible my brother had given me for college graduation. Scott had written some verses from the Old Testament inside its cover. The personal inscription he'd written to me was mostly in English, with a few Hebrew words thrown in for good measure. It read, in part:

> *Be brave, wise and alert, my sister.*
> *For you I have the pride of mountains,*
> *The* אהב *(love) of a mother,*
> *The hope of a father,*
> *The exuberance of a sister,*
> *The joy of angels,*
> *And the* חסד, *the steadfastness, of the ages.*

I could only assume that the foreign characters meant something good. Because I was interested in returning to do ministry in Camden, Scott had been encouraging me to consider attending seminary. The thought of learning Hebrew and Greek, though, completely repulsed me. The only Hebrew word I recognized in Scott's inscription was the word for love, אהב. After consulting him the previous summer, I'd actually had it shaved in the back of my head when I'd been a camp counselor in Camden. Hebrew, which uses no vowels, is a great language to use when shaving stuff into one's scalp. "Camp Victory" totally does not fit; my barber realized this after about six letters. He squeezed in a thin "c" and then there was no more head left. So *there's* one nice thing about Hebrew.

Now, as I searched for help in dealing with my jealousy, I flipped through my Bible and began scanning through Romans to find the passage that had drifted into my consciousness. Maybe, I hoped, it would offer me the comfort and wisdom I sought.

Flip. Flip. Flip. "If you live according to the flesh you will die . . . yada yada yada . . . For all who are led by the Spirit of God are children of God." I continued reading, "For you did not receive a spirit of slavery to fall back into fear, but you have received a spirit of adoption" (Romans 8:14-15).

My internal hard drive stopped spinning. I had never, in my whole entire Sunday school career, not to mention several college-level New Testament classes, seen the word *adoption* in Scripture. I understood the whole big idea about becoming God's own children, of course, but I'd never once seen the actual word *adoption* in the book. "When we cry, 'Abba! Father!'" the text continues, "it is that very Spirit bearing witness with our spirit that we are children of God" (Romans 8:15-16).

They just look like regular words when I read them now. In that holy moment, though, they rushed into the deep chasm in my center to fill the space that had been jostled open first by Isaiah's arrival and then wedged further by Pam's return. They were the sudden, unexpected answer to the question I hadn't realized I had been asking.

At first I couldn't figure out how I had never seen the word *adoption* in Scripture. On top of the impressive New Testament courses, Kelly and I had memorized the eighth chapter of Romans together. Memorized! If the word *adoption* had been in there, I think I would have known about it. What I was finally able to piece together, after a good deal of puzzling, was that the New International Version, which Kelly and I had memorized, says that God gives us a spirit of "sonship." The New Revised Standard Version that Scott had given me, though, uses the word "adoption." The discrepancy actually did give me my first wee little itch to learn Greek, because those two English words weren't even like apples and oranges. They were like apples and goats.

The previous week I'd been keenly aware that the "Who am I?" scribbled on the top of my to-do list had been answered in a powerful and serendipitous way. When Pam and I first spoke, who I was had suddenly seemed obvious as she told me of the faith, ministry, art and athletics that had been mine by birth. "Of course that's *already* who I am," I had decided. "I'm already the *me* I was made to be." The confirmation was reassuring. The words that I was hearing in the text of Romans, though, were now saying something different.

I don't throw "God spoke to me" language around lightly. Personal policy. Still, in those moments I heard God's voice more clearly than I had ever experienced it before. I'll borrow more language to say that a deep impression was made on my spirit. Though these aren't the exact words, I heard God say, "Margot, this is about me. All the hoopla about finding your roots is really about finding me. If you want to know who you are, turn this way. Look toward my face."

In that moment I was convicted that my primary identity had not, in fact, been transferred genetically through my bloodline, as I had deduced over the previous week. Suddenly it mattered little that I was creative or blue-eyed or tall. Though I had been begging God to answer the question "Who am I?" the question itself had been turned on its head, as *who* became *whose.*

When I had applied for a passport at age fourteen, I had been denied access to my original Massachusetts birth certificate. Instead, I had received a doctored one bearing the names of my adoptive parents. Even then I had thought it was fishy. When I found Pam, then I thought I'd stumbled on the ultimate *whose*, as if the birth-parent names I'd at last been given were the secret password unlocking access to my truest identity. In that prayerful encounter, however, the *divine* certification of whose I was, from the beginning of the world, had been steamed open. Now that this notarized documentation had been unsealed by the Spirit, I became convinced that I'd been sealed as God's own.

The vivification of those words from Romans, that I had been claimed by my Father, remains the single most powerful encounter with the Holy I have ever experienced.

After briefly marveling over that wonderful thing, I scampered off and started looking for my birth father.

J-Max

Curious, I glanced over the notes I'd jotted about Max from the conversation I'd had with Pam. He was an athlete, a cyclist and a runner, as well as an artist. The summer they met he had been earning money as a waiter. Pam thought his mother might have been a drum instructor at a local college. I sure liked the sound of that funky thing. Pam thought his Christian family had been Baptist but that his mother had converted to Catholicism. That little bit seemed to me even more edgy than being a drum teacher.

So much about who he was seemed to resonate with what I knew about myself. Although I had been born and adopted in Boston, my family moved to Illinois before my third birthday. The town where we lived until I graduated from high school was adjacent to my birth father's hometown. Surely we had competed on the same high school fields and ridden our bikes on the same streets. Pam recalled that Max's family had been actively involved in overseas missions. Like me. The summer I turned nineteen I had returned to Illinois to take a summer school course at Wheaton College where Max, too, had taken just one course. Typing for him, theology for me.

The trifecta of my natural curiosity, my hunger for relationship and my incredible gift for locating people pretty much guaranteed that I was going to find this guy. If he hoped for anonymity, which would have been a reasonable expectation when I was born, he didn't have a chance. I launched into the hunt with all the bravado of Indiana Jones.

On the inside, though, I was really more like that little cartoon bird who falls out of his nest in the children's book *Are You My Mother?* That newborn baby bird searches tirelessly for his mother, inquiring of all manner of farm animals and vehicles if they might be his. Finally, a steam shovel lifts the baby bird back up into its nest where it meets its mother. I eagerly hoped that, as I sleuthed around, I'd stumble on that gracious steam shovel, the one who would hoist me into my father's presence.

Nancy Drew Sleuthing

Pam had not kept in touch with Max. The last she had heard he was walking around California. As several decades had passed since then, I moved forward under the assumption that he was no longer walking around the state in which I now lived.

It seemed like the art angle might be the best way to find him. Abe, my boss at the bakery, was also a ceramics professor at University of California, Santa Barbara. He was the artiest guy in my life that year.

"So, Abe," I began hesitantly. "If I were trying to find someone who may or may not be an artist, and who may or may not be in California, and who may or may not be someplace in the United States, how might I go about it?" It seemed like a fairly straightforward question.

"Oh yeah," I added, "I don't exactly know if this person is alive. Let's assume he is."

Abe paused from cleaning the oven. "There's an annual index of art exhibits published in the magazine *Art in America*," he told me. "You could try there. The public library should have it. If they don't, it's at UCSB [University of California, Santa Barbara]."

And with that, my search had begun. A visit to the public library proved Abe to be right. I read there that Max had participated in a group show in Manhattan seven years earlier. More digging at the university yielded a few articles and several reproductions of Max's paintings of horses. One reviewer wrote, "To him, horses are not important as animals but as forms. He paints impersonally from matter-of-fact photographs that bear no trace of sentimentality."

No detail was without personal significance. *I drew horses for years when I was growing up!* I was obsessed with them. I have the drawings my grandmother had saved to prove it. I'd been scared of horses since age nine, however, when my Girl Scout troop went riding at a farm and a horse kicked me in the leg. As a result, I, too, was not the least bit sentimental about horses! Clearly we were cut from the same cloth.

Yet for every connection I could make, there was also a small clue that told me to beware. If he wasn't sentimental about horses, perhaps he wouldn't be sentimental about me either.

At the library I found several phone book listings in Manhattan for Max Edwards. In order to confirm which one belonged to *my* Max, I called the alumni office at a college he had attended and the name of which I'd gleaned from one of the library articles.

"I'm calling to find out how to contact Max Edwards. I would love to be in touch and I don't have a current address or phone number." I tried to sound sophisticated.

"And you are . . . ?" the voice on the other end queried.

I did not have a lie prepared. So I told the truth. Predictably, I was informed that they could not give out personal information like addresses or phone numbers. She didn't say, "Especially not to illegitimate love children," but I knew she was thinking it. Desperate, I decided to punt.

"Oh, I *know* where he lives." Apparently it wasn't that hard to lie after all.

"You do?" the voice asked, dubious.

I quickly scanned the four addresses I had copied from the New York phone books.

"Broome Street, right?" The street name matched one of the galleries that had hosted an exhibit.

"Yes," the voice confirmed. I decided from her tone that she secretly wanted to help me out.

"Sure, of course I know that." As my mouth kept moving, my mind raced to think of any more information I might be able to squeeze out of the alumni office.

Hesitantly, the woman queried, "You *do* know there are children involved?" It was a half-statement, half-question. Although she couldn't give out personal information, it might have been her way of saying, "Don't go barging in and messing up other people's lives."

I lied again. "Yeah, sure, I know." Wow. Siblings.

"Okay, then. Bye."

I wanted to say, "Thanks for your help," but I felt it would violate our unspoken agreement; that is, that she hadn't helped me. Even though we both knew she had.

The Telling

After Pam and I first spoke, I had called my dad, Rick, to fill him in and, as much as anything, to explain the weird phone call he'd received. Though surprised, he was supportive. My mom had been out of the country with her husband, Don, when it had all transpired. I was actually grateful for her absence, which gave me a week or so to gather my thoughts. For days I loved gushing the story to anyone who would lend me an ear. To my employers, friends and grocery clerks, it was like some fairy tale with a happy ending. I doubted it would sound quite as delightful to the mother who, until then, had had me all to herself.

I invited my mom to drive from her home in Santa Monica to meet me for lunch. She enjoyed Santa Barbara, and we chose an outdoor beach café. As we perused our menus, I felt uneasy. After we ordered, I clumsily began, "You know how you've always said you'd support me if I wanted to find my birth parents? Well . . ."

Eyes wide, she received my story. I was forthcoming with everything I knew about Pam and slightly more fuzzy about how driven I was to find Max. I don't think I even realized it myself. My mom was, understandably, a little guarded. She didn't want me to be hurt. I didn't want her to be hurt. In the end, she offered me her blessing. I thought it was very brave. After all, she didn't have any way of knowing what this new development would mean for our relationship. She didn't know whether or not things would change between us.

I knew. I knew that my mom was still my mom. What finding Pam and looking for Max *did* do was to remind me of all that my mom had done for me over the years. She'd nursed me through illness. She'd schooled me in the womanly ways of feminine hygiene. She'd dug with me through icky garbage cans to find each orthodontic retainer I'd accidentally thrown out. No new relationship would change any of that important stuff.

Gallery Opening

Although I now had Max's address, I was still too chicken to write him. Or call him. Or see him. All of these were much too risky. Although I never could have admitted that a rejection would sting, I think I must have known it in my gut. For the time being, I would continue to sleuth around and find out what I could.

The gallery was my next clue. During college I had worked in several art galleries. I knew that they often kept literature about previous shows, such as marketing postcards of an artist's work, tucked away in bulging file cabinet drawers.

I typed a letter to the gallery, careful to specify that I was interested in his "work," not him.

I am interested in the work of an artist you featured five or six years ago named Max Edwards. I would appreciate any information you could provide regarding his work. Thank you very much. Gratefully, Margot Starbuck

I included a self-addressed stamped envelope for good measure. I used fancy markers to make my name really colorful and pretty for extra good measure. The reply that arrived in my mailbox six weeks later was not signed by the gallery owner to whom I had addressed it.

The letter was signed: Max Edwards.

When the gallery had passed the letter along to him, Max wrote back, mistaking me for a patron of the arts. His letter, handwritten in black, felt-tip pen on white paper, began:

Dear Margot,

Your letter, dated March 22 arrived today—I was glad someone out there is so bold with interest and the letter arrived with such a fabulous envelope—so I'm writing back immediately. The return envelope is beautiful!

Do I know you?

It was kind of funny he should ask. The letter continued on to describe a few of the pieces he'd been working on. Then it continued:

I don't know if any of this makes sense so I'll send photos of anything you like.

Anything?

Thanks for the letter of interest.

Now that's an understatement.

Sincerely, Max Edwards

Although I'm clearly not beyond using a little imagination in my Nancy-Drew detective work, I never intended to misrepresent myself. So I began to compose the letter of a lifetime.

American Flag Stamp

I would have only one chance to make a good first impression. I wanted the letter to be perfect. Telling him he had bred me would need to be the hook at the beginning. To keep him reading. In the rest of the letter my plan was to make him interested, but not come off as too needy. There's nothing attractive about that.

So many choices had to be made. Tasteful floral stationery or plain white paper? Handwritten or typed? American flag postage stamp or a rainbow globe squished into the shape of a heart?

I decided that fancy stationery would communicate that I was trying too hard. At the same time, I couldn't pretend I was a plain white-paper girl. *That* would be a lie. I settled on a nice electric purple paper. As my penmanship left much to be desired, I typed. I would keep it business-like. *Definitely* an American flag stamp.

With no sort of salutation whatsoever, I just launched into it.

I can't think of a subtle way to do this, so: My name's Margot Starbuck
and I'm Pam's daughter. There, it's out.

I continued on to describe how Pam and I stumbled on each other
through the registry. Then I shared some stuff about me. Casual, I didn't
want it to sound like I was trying too hard.

Like any good cover letter, I kept it to one page.

That's it. I'm sure you have a family and a real life now, and I don't
want to disrupt that. What can I say? Thanks for the great genes. I
guess the ball's in your court. I really do respect whatever decision you
make.

Margot

At the time I truly thought that I meant what I said about respecting
whatever decision he made. I just didn't realize that he would make the
decision not to contact me.

After a month of waiting to get a response, I couldn't take it anymore;
I had to know what he was thinking. So I folded a piece of paper—white
this time—into fourths like a little folding note card. On the front I car-
tooned a dead cat. On its back. Feet sticking up in the air. I drew Xs
where his little feline eyes should have been. Because nothing says "I
can take you or leave you" like a dead cat.

Below the image I wrote, "Curiosity killed the cat."

When the card was opened, there was another simple cartoon of
me—glasses, chin-length hair, stripy denim overalls—with a little word
bubble that read simply, "Meow."

If purple paper and a typewriter hadn't won his affection the first
time, perhaps the boring white paper, handwriting and graphics would.
I also switched it up and used tulip stamps.

Tucked inside was a 3 x 5 card with simple instructions. These read
as follows:

Your response is requested by simply returning one of the enclosed response cards. (Humor me.)

A. *Yes, I received your letter and have chosen not to respond at this time.*

B. *Yes, I received your letter but am trapped under a heavy object and am unable to respond at this time.*

C. *Yes, I received your letter and have been so busy planning the reunion I haven't found time to contact you.*

D. *I have no idea what you're talking about. Please elaborate.*

Thank-you for your time.
With all due respect,
[Signed Margot]
M. Starbuck

Included were four plain, stamped postcards simply labeled A, B, C and D. I used *both* a flowery "Margot" signature and a more business-like, typed one: "M. Starbuck." I desperately hoped that one of them would appeal.

Max wrote back later that week. Exactly 402 words. The letter was kind, informative, revealing. It answered a lot of my questions, and it hatched others. One-half of his family tree included a rich history of Christian ministry, evangelism and scholarship. The other side was active in theater, vaudeville and film. It really did explain so much.

In closing, Max indicated that he'd be willing to meet with me when I was on the East Coast but that we should put our relationship on hold for the time being. I could live with that.

In the next day's mail I received one of my reply postcards. D. At first I didn't think it was very well-chosen, because he really did know what I was talking about, but I could see how it was a better fit than any of the other three. Scrawled in pencil across my big D was the message:

Margot, Just tell me something about yourself—no graphics.

Hooray! And ouch.

Desperately Not Desperate

If I had thought the first letter was hard, this one felt equally weighty. That's why I began it:

I feel like I'm applying for a scholarship. (My essay is called "A Little Something About Myself . . .")

I continue on to describe my perfect Margot Cleaver life. It was printed by hand on lined school paper. Because I hadn't tried that writing paper option yet.

I grew up in Glen Ellyn. My parents were divorced when I was six, and after a second difficult marriage my mom married my eye doctor, moved to Santa Monica and has lived happily ever after. This means I have a number of wonderful parents and a great family. My grandmother taught me how to sew and paint, my grandfather taught me how to ride a bike and drive a car, and my brother taught me how to shine his football cleats and start his car in the winter.

I was fortunate enough to have some special friends, too. Our time was spent lollygagging, eating pizza and dancing in parking lots. My best friend, Mindy, and I would sew matching bike shorts, ride to Fermilab in Naperville, and take our easels and watercolors to paint the buffalo there. I've written stories and made videos of the grand road trip adventures Mindy and I have had in twenty-six states and four countries.

I really did squeeze biking and painting into the same sentence, didn't I? I was trying too hard.

In 1987 I began college at Westmont where for the first time I saw peers living different lives because they knew Christ. That was a challenge to me and for the last five years knowing and loving God has been my greatest desire.

Corita Kent is the biggest influence on the series of posters I showed in my senior art show last May. The ideas were generated from experiences in the inner-city of Camden, New Jersey, where I lived nine months over the last two years. I wanted my art to be a voice for the oppressed. I think my art professors would have been happier if I'd written a book about the ills of society and let art be art.

In October my roommate Geni had a little baby boy named Isaiah (with my video camera in his face from birth). When he was tiny I'd look at this little bundle of molecules and think, "He is just ½ mom and ½ dad." (Since he hadn't developed his own little self yet.) And I realized— I'm ½ someone. So I sent in the form and the rest is history. I wasn't on a desperate hunt for more parents, but it has been a grand adventure.

Can't you see, Max, how *not* desperate I am? I was desperately not desperate.

This year I'm delivering bread, working in a senior citizen daycare center and caring for an elderly lady. I also work with the high school kids at church and am the artist for a nonprofit newsletter for kids with cancer. Needless to say I feel very blessed. After/during graduate school I hope to pass that on by investing myself in a community like Camden. Thank you for writing, Max. I can tell you have a lot on your heart and mind right now. Hang in there.

Margot

P.S. Before I wrote, I tried to put myself in your position—but I didn't know what that was. Now that I know a bit I can begin to imagine what an untimely burden this could be.

We were probably both thinking the same thing. Not what a burden *"this"* could be but rather what a burden *"I"* am. I was thinking it, anyway.

Put it out of your mind for now.

Even though I wrote it, I didn't really mean it. Unfortunately, he called my bluff.

I knew in my gut that Max did not want to be in a relationship with me. Though it felt too harsh to volunteer that information to perfect strangers, I did feel obligated to share it with those who had journeyed with me as the story unfolded. When I had to say it, I framed it all kinds of ways. "What a shock," I'd report with understanding. "Of course, he already *has* a life," I'd explain. "It's a lot to take in," I'd offer empathetically. Bottom line, of course, was that he didn't want me. Again. And that was not something *I* was prepared to take in. Again. So I continued to believe that after the shock wore off, he would come to his senses and want me. Love always hopes.

Two people in my life knew how hurtful Max's rejection was before I did. (On second thought, I suspect that *everybody* knew how hurtful it was before I did.) The ones I remember speaking it to me were Pam and my dad, Rick. I could see how they ached for me to be received. Neither one had anything particular to gain from Max turning toward me with open arms; if anything, they were at risk of losing a little of me. Each, of course, had been in Max's shoes. Faced with me, they chose something else. For reasons that were much bigger than me, they had each left me. Neither one wanted to see me rejected again.

Reunion

Pam and I finally met face to face in July. She bought me a plane ticket to visit her in the homeland, Boston. Because I flew out of Los Angeles, I did all the last-minute prep at my mom and Don's home in Santa Monica. My mom helped me with all my packing and primping.

By the time I boarded the airplane, just after midnight, I looked like Tammy Faye Bakker. Only with bigger hair. I can't even blame it on my mom. Somehow I'd taken all my nervous energy and thrown it into clothes, hair and makeup. I really wanted to impress.

I landed in Boston at ten in the morning. I looked around nervously for Pam. Would I recognize her from the photos she'd sent? Would she know me? I had to smile when I finally spotted her checking the posted listings of incoming flights. Her long, straight, brown hair hung past her shoulders. We were the same height. Her body curved in and out in all the same places mine did. Looking a little lost, she was padding around the airport in faded blue jeans and crazy red tennis shoes. I suddenly felt silly for getting all dolled up. I simply pointed at her shoes and blurted, "That's exactly what I *usually* look like!"

It had quickly become entirely obvious where half my DNA had come from.

After we left the airport we tooled around the city with Pam's husband, Stan, and ate lunch at Boston's historic Quincy Market. When we finally arrived at their home, exhausted, I took a very long nap. Just like a newborn.

Pam and I packed a lot into our long weekend. We strolled through the Public Garden. We ate way too much food at some great restaurants. We perused albums of family photos. We visited an exhibit of Annie Leibovitz's photography. Inspired, Pam and I returned to her home and snapped shots of our hands and feet. The roll of film revealed what no photo that included me ever had.

We matched.

Running for No Particular Reason

The week Isaiah was born, the last week of October, I had started running.

What made that particularly strange was that five years earlier I had made a vow to never run again. More often than not, I'm a person of my word.

Every Friday in junior high each able-bodied student at Hadley Junior High School had been required to run a complicated mile through woods and fields. Not one week passed that I did not dread the run. When I got to high school I had to run because I was on the basketball and track teams. I'll admit that the running requirement for the track team should have been a no-brainer, but I had secretly hoped there was some sort of waiver for those of us lugs competing only in the discus throw and shot put. Sadly, the state-mandated gym class runs also continued in high school. I have a clear memory of the day when, as a senior, I ran the last timed mile of my entire gym class career. While other seventeen-year-olds were still dreaming of so many of life's firsts, I was relishing the fact that this would be the last time I'd have to run. Much to my dismay, I was required to do it my first year of college too. That's right, I was *paying* to run.

I hope you can see how it was a teensy-weensy bit strange that I began running for sport the very week that Isaiah was born, for no particular reason. I had cycled to the beach, leaving my bike, shoes and socks by the road. Crossing the cool morning sand of the volleyball courts, I began by running along the water from the end of East Beach to the East Beach Bar and Grill. The distance was about a quarter mile, max. The next day I ran all the way to the traffic light at Milpas Street. The day after that I ran as far as the traffic light beyond Milpas Street. It was like some weird fitness miracle. I did it one week, then two, then three, then four.

Although I'd always kept healthy by roller skating to groovy 1970s songs and by riding my yummy rainbow-painted bike, the running completely stunned me. Still wondering about it, a month after Isaiah was born I'd written in my journal, asking it of the universe, "Why am I doing this?"

In *Forrest Gump*, after being abandoned by his true love, Jenny, Forrest stands up from a rocker on his porch and begins to run. His narrative voiceover announces, "That day, for no particular reason, I decided to go for a little run." When Forrest reaches the end of the driveway, he turns and runs down the highway. At the end of the road he decides he will run to the end of town. At the end of town he decides to run through Greenbow County. Then, since he has run that far, he thinks he might just run across the great state of Alabama.

"For no particular reason," explains Forrest, "I just kept going. I ran clear to the ocean."

Me too.

Running on Empty

From the moment I learned about Max, I longed to identify with him. Although I had always been more of a graphic artist than a painter, I immediately pulled out my paints and created a portrait of Max from one of the photos Pam had sent. When I wasn't running on the beach I was racing my cool bike down State Street imagining I was in the Tour de France. Because Max's grandfather had been a scholar of classic languages, I actually got it in my head that a natural affinity for languages had been preprogrammed on my hard drive. No wonder French and Spanish had come so easily in high school and college! I didn't waste one more single minute of dread worrying about taking Greek or Hebrew. In a word, I was empowered.

Four months after Isaiah was born, I was still running. Just like Forrest. It was as if Isaiah's entry had unleashed a pent-up energy that just had to find release. The fact that, in February, I learned from Pam that Max had been a runner only confirmed that I'd chosen the *right* release.

As I continued to run, it began to feel like flying. When one foot left the ground, I felt the way cheetahs look when a camera snaps them in midair. Sometimes I would retrace my steps just to confirm that the footprints were *really* as far apart as I imagined them on the NBC Sports reel that ran through my mind. With visions of barefoot South African runner Zola Budd dancing in my head, I pretended that I, too, was a champion. Had I known about my rich heritage sooner, I reasoned, I would most likely be competing in the International Olympic Games that very summer.

I slowly began to suspect that neither Forrest nor I had been running for "no particular reason" after all. There *was* a reason our feet had been set in hopeless motion. I still recall the feeling I experienced during the movie when Forrest's Jenny glances up at a television during her waitressing shift to notice the news coverage of Forrest's cross-country run. When she does, she sees Forrest. They had not been in contact since she left him six or seven years earlier. A wave of relief washed over me when I realized that he'd at last been *seen*. If I had been in the Olympics that summer, maybe the one for whom my heart pined would have seen me too.

When people run through the soft, deep, volleyball-court sand on the beach, it's good exercise. Running barefoot on wet, hard-packed sand at water's edge, though, is just stupid. I know that now. Yet that's exactly what I did day after day, week after week, month after month. When my heels began to throb, I ignored the discomfort. No pain, no gain, right? When the front of my foot began to ache, I ignored it. I had avoided pain for twenty-two years, and I had no plans to start facing it now.

By the end of the summer, I had been running for nine months. I'd been in pain for more than half of those. Eventually the light pressure on my feet when I was in a sitting position brought me to tears. The pain of rejection that my heart had refused was being made manifest in my body.

It was as if someone, somewhere, was trying to tell me to stop running after that Max.

-five-

WELCOME TO OZ

Choosing to be with Geni, Terry and Isaiah after graduation meant that the grand opening of my life—the one in which I was all self-actualized—had been postponed a year. It never once occurred to me that the baby boy who had forever changed me might have held me right in place simply by virtue of his wonderfulness. I had no category for it.

With the exception of Geni and Bug, my friends from that year were all moving in different directions. I, though, continued to dream about living in urban America. The mental snapshot I'd concocted of this fabulous life featured me hanging out near a dumpster with homeless women. It wasn't everyone's dream life, but it was mine. Bred Presbyterian, I knew that I would need to attend seminary before going into full-time ministry. You wouldn't want to let someone loose among the poor without a graduate degree.

With the exception of confusing it with a monastery at age fifteen, I had little experience with an actual seminary. I had visited Scott just once at Princeton Seminary while he was studying things with icky names like exegesis and Ugaritic. My friend Bruce, from Camden, had been finishing up his M.Div. at Princeton the previous fall, and I'd helped him film a video for one of his classes. In it, he'd invited Camden kids to rap gospel stories to a funky urban beat. How cool was that? What with my experience producing Isaiah's birth video, I just *knew* I could be the best seminary student ever.

I also heard a few things from Kyle, a youth pastor with whom I'd served in Santa Barbara. When he was a student at Fuller Seminary, he and all his friends had sat outside in lawn chairs during a thunderstorm to clap and cheer when the sky exploded with lightning. "Yay, God!" they'd hollered. Upon hearing this I had reasoned, "I could go to seminary. I really could. I could do that."

Clapping and cheering and rapping sounded way more fun than Ugaritic. Despite Scott, both Fuller and Princeton seminaries quickly climbed to the top of my list of potential graduate schools.

Theological Camps

Noticing different flavors of Christians around me, I began considering where I stood theologically. Among the many Christians I respected, there was no hint of homogeneity. Rather, I noted insightfully in my blue notebook, there were three kinds: "Father Christians," "Son Christians" and "Spirit Christians." That year I felt like I needed to choose for myself among those three Neapolitan stripes that had somehow gotten squeezed together in one Christian box.

According to my painfully artificial schema, the "Father Christians" had a great respect for the awesomeness of God—and I don't mean that in the surfer sense of the word. Scott was one of these. He cautioned me against behaving as if I could just pick up the phone and talk to God, when that's *exactly* what I wanted to do. His counsel came from a deep respect for the holiness and majesty of the God of the Israelites who called David his son.

The "Son Christians" were all about pursuing relationships with Christ and with each other. Being in relationship with Jesus Christ was always being fleshed out in relationship to others. Kelly and Jane were part of this Jesus-y fellowship.

The "Spirit Christians" were the pick-up-the-phone types. Our friend Rhonda, from Geni's cool interracial, Holy Spirit church, was one of these. She actually *heard* stuff from God. I don't mean that she gleaned inspiration from the pages of the Holy Writ. I mean that when she was walking past the laundromat a voice told her to turn left. You can imagine how attractive that was for someone who was listening for theological answers. Keenly interested, I moonlighted at Geni's church when I could steal away from mine. One Sunday I was re-baptized there, but then felt really bad about it. Because I'm Presbyterian.

My future, if not the heavenly one then certainly the terrestrial one, hung in the balance. If I decided to be a "Father Christian," I would go to Princeton or Fuller. Problem solved. If I decided to be a "Son Christian," I would flesh out the Christlike life with Kelly and Jane. Problem solved. The best possible scenario would have been ending up as a "Spirit Christian," because then God would just tell me what to do in my ear. And that would be great, of course.

I was in a knot about how to understand my faith when all the people I respected so much understood theirs so differently. I had spent most of my life pleasing adults and keeping them happy, as insurance that they wouldn't leave me. Although the routine had served me well, it failed the moment I became unable to please everyone at once. Otherwise, I would have kept at it. I actually had a page in my journal that reads:

If _____ weren't around, I would _____ .

It was kind of like Mad Libs for people pleasers. Then I listed each person's name and how I would be freed up if I wasn't living to please

them. Or if, "their-God" forbid, they suffered some horrible accident. It
went something like this:

> If _Scott_ weren't around, I would _not be considering Princeton._
> If _Bruce_ weren't around, I would _not be in such a hurry to get to_
> _Camden._
> If the _Presbyterian Church_ weren't around, I would _join Geni's_
> _groovy interracial, Holy Spirit church._

You get the idea.

The conundrum was constantly spinning through my mind. Since
those Father-ish Presbyterians loved learning, I had the thought one
morning in the bathroom, "If I respond to the _Spirit_ and go to Maryland
with Jane and Kelly to _learn_ to be a disciple of _Jesus,_ I might just make
everyone happy."

No sooner had I thought it than I remembered my grandfather, who
had encouraged me to continue my formal education: "_Oh no!_ Grand-
dad! Rats!" In my experience, people raised during the Depression have
very little appreciation for intentional Christian lifestyles that do not
involve paychecks.

If I really wanted to clear my head and listen for God's leading, I was
going to need to let go of all of these influences. This was easier said
than done. At one point in the process I mentally rounded up every last
one of these influential people and marched them onto an imaginary
airplane. Row after row of the virtual jumbo jet was filled with those
that I loved and whose faith I respected.

Then I imagined it crashing into the earth where it exploded into a
ball of flames.

Weird and creepy, huh? I know. If you're a people pleaser, though,
you understand.

During that perplexing season, I received a note in the mail from

Bruce. He was traveling in the Northwest and jotted me a note on a comment card he'd picked up at a new little coffee shop called Starbucks. His comments read as follows:

> *Go to Princeton, keep your hands covered with the muck of the world, refine your obvious gifts, learn to become a clear and sharp thinker, develop a broader view of the church and her history, inject some reality into the hollow arguments of the theologians, keep your wonderful spirit and life outlook, live in Camden and commute to school.*

It's what would finally push me over the edge to choose to attend Princeton Theological Seminary.

An Unexpected Rupture

The day Geni and Isaiah drove me to the airport for my flight east, I didn't anticipate an emotional parting. Although I had seen my grandfather fight back tears when he said goodbye to me at the end of our visits, I've never been one for sappy farewells. Having decided early on that I would not be saddled with the pain of separation, I typically felt nothing.

Other than the occasional funeral, the times when I really needed to squeeze out a few tears to appear socially respectable were the last few minutes of the summer at Camp Miniwanca. After the closing council circle, hundreds of girls would dissolve into weeping as we said our goodbyes. Usually, in those moments, I tried to think of something really sad—well, something that *would* be sad if I had feelings. Imagining the eventual loss of my steadfast grandmother was usually my old standby. Even at the time I'd thought it odd that, searching for the most excruciating loss I could imagine, my mind turned to her. Losing a parent was just too . . . well, imaginable. My insides were already steeled against it.

Posing with Geni and Isaiah on the breezy tarmac of the Santa Barbara airport, before I gave my grandmother a thought, I was grinning from ear to ear for our final family photo. Had it only been ten months since I'd driven Geni to the hospital? It felt like a lifetime. Hugging that precious boy, and the mother who had kept him, I offered a rote smile for the camera, fortified against feelings as I'd been so many times before. I had no reason to expect that this round of goodbyes would be any different than the many—and I do mean many—that I had already endured.

Yet as I took my window seat, the ten-month crack in my heart's armor suddenly burst open. Unexpected tears gave way to heaving sobs as my undoing shook the small plane. I came completely unglued. Seven words pounded relentlessly in my head. The deep question for which I was without an answer, the one I had never dared to ask, echoed inside me: *How could a parent leave a child?*

Welcome to Oz

Thankfully, the whirring activity of orientation kept my mind mostly off of Isaiah. I had decided to begin seminary in the dorm, rather than in Camden, in order to meet people and jump into life in my new community. On the second or third night, the seminary president gathered all the first-year students together in the campus dining hall. After introducing his staff, he proceeded to introduce his "dear, sweet wife." Typically enamored and a little surprised by men who were affectionate with their wives, I found his introduction of his wife dear. And sweet. Following the convocation, on the walk back to our dorm, I discovered that I was pretty much alone on that one.

"It made my stomach churn," one fellow student offered. More echoed their agreement. The overall consensus was one of unmitigated disgust.

That's when it hit me: "Toto, we are not in Kansas anymore." Not only was I no longer in the Midwest *or* California, I had definitely arrived in Oz.

I had kerplopped into a whole new galaxy from the Christian community I had experienced in Santa Barbara. If I thought it was funny that my college in California was supposed to have *tamed* me after high school, it was wackier still that I had to *leave* southern California to be exposed to such a wide diversity of ideas about patriarchy, gender, sexuality, theology and language.

In this strange new world, it seemed to me that men were held suspect simply by virtue of having been born male. The ones who had played football in high school, married young, gone into ministry and espoused traditional family values were thought by some to be the worst kind. Disdain for the *wives* of many of these more theologically conservative male students, the women who cooked their dinners and typed their papers, was undisguised. Now see, back in Santa Barbara, that whole "living-for-the-other" situation was exactly what we were going for.

It was a hard place for someone who had negotiated emotional survival by avoiding conflict. That said, I don't want to make it sound like it was hard for me and easy for everyone else to live and study and worship in that theologically and socially diverse community. It wasn't. I heard the same thing from almost every student I met: female and male, liberal and conservative, young and old, U.S. citizen and international student, feminist and nonfeminist, straight and gay, premillennialist and postmillennialist, black and white, Latino and Asian, and all the other people groups that don't even get mentioned in a list like this. Many had confessed to feeling a little bit like a fish out of water that year at Princeton Seminary.

You know you're probably in Oz when white American males feel marginalized.

Pain Management

The one thing that remained consistent during my intergalactic transition
was the pain in my feet. If nothing else, that pain was dependable. Because I had been waiting to be covered by my student insurance policy
before seeking treatment for my feet, one of the first things I did was to
make an appointment with a physician at Princeton University. The diag-
nosis was a no-brainer: plantar fasciitis. In this fairly common running
injury, the fascia, the connective tissue that runs along the bottom of the
foot, is damaged through injury or overuse. That doctor sent me to a
sports medicine guy. He told me to take pain medication and do some
sort of hot and cold thing before and after exercise. Or was it cold and hot?
Whatever it was, I quickly grew bored of it. Avoiding life's pain had worked
for me until then just fine, thank you. So I put it out of my mind and kept
going. I could no longer run, but I did walk and ride my bike. And, of
course, I took the train. Into Manhattan. Which is where Max lived.

Though I had sent Max my new school address, he had not responded.
I was disappointed but not surprised. Neither his disinterest, however,
nor the fifty-one miles separating us were nearly enough to thwart my
curiosity. Though I was too scared to risk attempting a real relationship,
one that involved actual dialogue, I was not at all above sneaky spying.
One day a friend and I took the train into Manhattan and caught a sub-
way to Greenwich Village. As we pushed our way through bustling sidewalks I became keenly aware that Max and I were probably breathing
the same air, as we'd most likely done unaware in Illinois. My eyes darted
from face to face to see if any of them looked familiar. Besides my own,
the only images I had upon which to base my speculations were the
photos Pam had given me from the summer of love. I mentally tried to
age Max's twenty-four-year-old face by twenty-three years. Whether or
not I'd come up with a reasonable approximation, I simply felt in my
heart that I would *know* him.

It wasn't difficult to find the address to which I'd written six months earlier. My friend and I positioned ourselves to wait at an outside café across the street from the building. The best possible scenario would have been for Max to come out. Or go in. Given my druthers I would have chosen out. So that we could follow him, of course.

Ostensibly it should have been difficult to gain entrance to the locked apartment building—*if* we had not been so super-helpful to the handymen who were trying to get a very long and unwieldy ladder out the front door. Because our original plan had not included breaking and entering—or helping and entering, for that matter—we didn't know exactly what to do once we were in there. My friend and I anxiously climbed the narrow staircase to the fourth floor where I was able to view Max's very own door. It was the one he probably walked through every day.

My friend wanted me to pose in front of Max's apartment for a picture, but I just couldn't do it. Max might have been *in* there! What if he heard us giggling and, heaven forbid, opened the door? Because then we would have seemed kind of stalker-ish. Even if I *was* a stalker I had no intention of Max knowing it. Snapping a quick picture of an awfully plain brown door, we fled down the steps like cockroaches scurrying back into our dark roachy crevices.

In the first letter Max had sent after he knew I was me, he suggested that we could get together when I was on the East Coast. I had doubted from the beginning we ever would. I know I could have picked up the phone and called, but I was too scared. After all, he might have *answered* it.

Exclusive Language

The challenge of finding words to speak to an earthly father was rivaled only by choosing ones for a heavenly father. Choosing language for God, yet another new frontier for me, was a big deal at Princeton. School policy required using inclusive language for God and human beings in our coursework. Although learning how to write and say stuff like "God is who God says that God is" felt a little clunky at first, I caught on pretty quickly.

As a woman who had never seen any limits to what I could achieve or accomplish, not to mention the award-winning inspirational sermons about not sacrificing one's self for a guy, I had naturally assumed I was already pretty enlightened. Gradually, though, I began to see how my language exposed the way that I thought. No, I didn't think that God was a man, but some of the subtleties of my language turned out to be revealing.

One day at dinnertime I plunked my tray down at a cafeteria table where a second-year woman was defending the use of male language for God to the dismay of a man who, like me, had just begun at the school. He, however, was already up to speed. Apparently he'd been paying attention when they covered this stuff at his fancy Ivy League school. And so it was that the first lively conversation about feminism to which I was personally privy was between a feminist male and a nonfeminist female. One month earlier I hadn't even known that there were such Earth creatures. I just listened quietly. Part of the reason was that I still had so much to learn. The other reason was that I was afraid. Of conflict.

Another woman I met was completely opposed to the word *wife*. While I'll be the first person to admit that there can be some pretty crazy baggage with both the word and the actual job description, I was still a little shocked. It was, to me, equally as troubling as the pursuit of an MRS degree. Despite the woman's rejection of the word, the woman *did* plan to be married one day. How would I refer to her? I thought that "spousal humanoid with vagina" had a nice ring.

I often felt a little on edge in conversations during those first months because there were so many potential landmines. Some were legitimate; others were just silly. If I needed to be schooled on issues of gender or race, I was more than willing to open my mind and learn something. I was not, however, thrilled about being corrected for calling the path running along a nearby canal the "bike path." It was, I was curtly informed, for walking, running *and* biking.

Being so inclusive could get a little exhausting.

Women and Men

My friend Jody could see I needed help getting up to speed. A recent graduate of Calvin College, she recommended a book called *Gender & Grace* by a Christian feminist there, Mary Stewart Van Leeuwen. In one chapter, based on the account of the Fall in Genesis, Van Leeuwen suggests that men and women may naturally be tempted toward sin in different ways. Men, she suggests, are tempted to turn the responsibility of dominion into domination, while women are tempted to turn sociability into social enmeshment. Although I was admittedly a gender-issues rookie, her assessment rang true.

At the same time I was exploring Van Leeuwen, one of my professors, James Loder, was teaching about Paul's riff in Galatians about being crucified with Christ.

> *I have been crucified with Christ; and it is no longer I who live, but it is Christ who lives in me. And the life I now live in the flesh I live by faith in the Son of God, who loved me and gave himself for me. (Galatians 2:19-20)*

I was captivated by the way Loder described the dynamic of the "I" and "Not I" relationship of which Paul spoke. Christ's residence in human hearts, Loder explained, put to death the ego-driven "I." The result was that those who had lived with a fear of abandonment were freed up to love because Christ, residing in human hearts, is the One who never leaves or forsakes. Similarly, those who feared absorption were liberated via the wellspring of Christ's own love that was at work in and through them. That great news enthralled me.

I also thought it provided a great complement to Van Leeuwen's assessment of gender differences. Christ's residence in human hearts could liberate and transform both those tempted toward enmeshment, who are often but not always female, and also those tempted toward domination, who are often but not always male.

I never made a peep about my suspicion that Christ's work in masculine and feminine hearts could be in any way distinct or unique. As I quietly listened to conversations around cafeteria tables, I wasn't hearing any dialogue on legitimate *differences* between men and women. Neither did I feel particularly equipped to initiate one. I suspected the silence I perceived was because, historically, difference has so often threatened equality between the sexes. It is an admittedly slippery slope.

Although I was not yet able to articulate it well, I was certain that there was treasure in store for the church in celebrating the unique gifts of women. Toward this end, for my master's thesis, I surveyed feminist women about the unique gifts and strengths, differences and similarities, between women and men. I gave each woman a list of questions to answer. In response to an inquiry about physical differences, one woman, normally a very sharp thinker, wrote, "There are no physical differences between men and women."

The Naughty "F" Word

The place where gender, theology and language intersected was right at the F word. That's right: *Father.* I even feel a little nervous writing it now. If YHWH had been the unspeakable name of God to the ancient Hebrews, FTHR was the modern counterpart on my campus.

Traditional "Father" language for God carried with it, for many, the residue of centuries of patriarchy in the church and in society. To have used it in a public service of worship, such as in the seminary chapel, would have offended and excluded many from worshiping freely. Maybe most. The few who dared to use it included the seminary president, most international students, and a handful of foolhardy conservatives. Not me.

It suddenly struck me as funny that when I had been assigning people to theological camps, I'd pegged the Presbyterian scholarly types as the "Father Christians." I realized now that the "Son Christians" and "Spirit Christians" I knew—daring to chat with God as Father and even using the occasional daring "Dad"—were much bigger Father-ists than anyone I met in the academy.

As someone who was still stinging with the recent rejection of an earthly father, I found myself in quite a spiritual pickle. During the season when I most needed to turn to a gracious heavenly Father, that very expression of God's nature had been called into question. The Father of Jesus, for some, was nothing more than a good-for-nothing man who subjected his child to bloody abuse. Add to that the centuries of subjugation of women and children, and I could begin to see why some people were not all that jazzed about "Father" language.

I, though, still hungered for a Father who was good. As I turned my face toward God's for comfort, I longed to be seen, known and loved by a Father who would look at me and accept me as I was. No one expressly forbade me to relate to God as Father in the quiet of my heart. Looking back, it would have been great if I could have found strength and comfort from a gracious Father God in my private devotions. I didn't.

It was unfortunate that before I even got to seminary I had divvied up God into neat thirds. Now even those pieces had split in two. Trust me when I say that there is little comfort to be gleaned from a Trivial Pursuit pie-piece God.

That year a gracious Father in heaven seemed just about as far away as the one who lived fifty-one miles from me.

A New Logic

A few folks from my church in Santa Barbara had warned me about Princeton. As in the era of the medieval European explorers who had set off over the horizon in search of new lands, only to lose their lives to the sea, rumors of doom and despair abounded. It wasn't that I would die during my passage, of course; it was worse. More than one student, I was informed, had set off for America's East Coast, landed at Princeton Seminary and lost their faith. When naysayers regaled me with these ecclesial ghost stories, I was polite enough, but I didn't believe it was going to happen.

Their doomsday forecast was, however, the reason that I was taken off-guard by the inspiring lectures from my fabulous professor, Dr. James Loder. I use *fabulous* here not to indicate that he was a brilliant educator—which in fact he was—but to communicate something even better than that. In an introductory psychology class he told us the story of his own near-death experience and encounter with the Holy Spirit. The tears running down his face were about the Spirit part, not the death part. And how cool is that? Even as a noncrier, I loved it that he cried.

Loder, traveling with his family, had stopped to help two women change a tire by the side of the road. As Loder was working under the car, a passing truck driver fell asleep at the wheel and hit the car; my professor was dragged through the gravel and trapped beneath the car. His physically small wife lifted the car off of him, freeing him from the bind. Just like in the Incredible Hulk.

Loder explained, "As I roused myself from under the car, a steady surge of life was rushing through me carrying with it two solid assur-

ances. First, I knew how deeply I felt love for those around me, especially my family. . . . The second assurance was that this disaster had a
purpose. . . . Walking from the car to the embankment, I never felt more
conscious of the life that poured through me, nor more aware that this
life was not my own."*

Five Easy Steps!

That experience of the Holy, which had reordered both Loder's personal
life and his intellectual one, is what he came to call a *transforming moment*. When he told the story in class, I recognized immediately that he
had identified what I had experienced nine months earlier. In relation to
the text of the eighth chapter of Romans, my prayerful encounter with a
divine Father had reordered my own experience. The fact that I had
quickly become wrapped up in a search to identify with a human father
did not negate the fact that I had been claimed by Another. In his book
The Transforming Moment: Understanding Convictional Experience, Loder
proposes a logic, or grammar, of the Holy Spirit in relation to the human
spirit.** It goes something like this:

1. A conflict occurs, also known as a "double bind."

2. After that comes an interlude of scanning for solutions.

3. At some point there's an "Aha!" insight, or constructive act of the
   imagination.

4. After that comes a release of pent-up energy.

5. Eventually, the knower comes to an interpretation of the experience
   that is tested publicly.

---

*James Loder, *The Transforming Moment: Understanding Convictional Experience* (Colo-
rado Springs: Helmers & Howard, 1989), p. 10.
**Ibid., pp. 58-60.

This is the logic, claims Loder, that is at work within both the Holy and the human spirits. He brings in lots of other really brainy hypotheses and research and philosophers, but this was the part I understood, in my bones.

I'm as big a fan of "five easy steps" as the next gal. Unfortunately, Loder's rubric was not that simple. What made it a little trickier was that there was not necessarily a linear progression from conflict through interpretation. That would be too easy. Instead, the transformational logic could be entered into at any point.

In my case, of course, I'd lived for twenty-two great years without any conflict over the dissonance of my experience. Relinquishment? Violence? Alcoholism? Divorce? There were just a lot of people who loved me. No conflict there, so no solution was needed.

So basically, *despite* me, the sudden and compelling insight in response to Romans 8—that I had been claimed as God's own—became the station at which I had hopped on board the Spirit train. Or rather, was taken up by it. The logic of the Spirit that Loder had articulated allowed me to see beyond the compelling "Aha!" insight to recognize the Spirit's larger movement in my heart, head, muscles and bones.

My renewed interest in painting, the Olympic Games and Tour de France fantasies, the release of my Greek and Hebrew learning anxieties, and of course the running and more running, were all ways that I was releasing the pent-up energy I didn't even know I was carrying. Just like Forrest. That semester I was at last able to interpret, to test and to make public what I had experienced. I wrote a fabulous term paper for Dr. Loder, and I also had the opportunity to tell my story to a fellowship group on campus.

I didn't know exactly when I would cycle back to those pesky first two points—the conflict and the scanning for solutions—but I was in no rush. Bearing the anxiety bound up in a conflict that didn't yet have a resolution would've been too hard. Plus, when you've started with dessert, who wants to go back and eat the vegetables?

Deconstructionist Reading

Although I would not claim it with the same fervor that I had for that great adoption passage in Romans, another biblical text gripped me that year. It snuck up on me when I was reading through the Prophets for Old Testament class. I felt certain that I had never heard it read in worship and I won't even pretend that I'd read it myself in *any* version of the Bible. If the message of Romans had put together the pieces of my experience in a meaningful way, Ezekiel was about to do a little dismantling.

Ezekiel was one of God's tireless prophets chosen for the job of announcing to Israel her sin. It wasn't a real popular job. As the sixteenth chapter opens, the prophet speaks to Israel the words that the Lord has put in his mouth, weaving an allegory about Israel's unfaithfulness. Before Ezekiel gets to the bad news, though, there is a fantastic bit about a child God loves who was born out of wedlock.

I decided to use the text for preaching class. The day I was to deliver my first sermon to other students in the class, in Princeton's historic Miller Chapel, I got all gussied up in mom-bought clothes, penny loafers *and* makeup. I was all ready to preach my little heart out.

> Your origin and your birth were in the land of the Canaanites; your father was an Amorite, and your mother a Hittite. (Ezekiel 16:3)

That, I explained to my class, was the ancient way of calling someone illegitimate.

> As for your birth, on the day you were born your navel cord was not cut, nor were you washed with water to cleanse you, nor rubbed with salt, nor wrapped in cloths. No eye pitied you, to do

any of these things for you out of compassion for you; but you were thrown out in the open field, for you were abhorred on the day you were born. (Ezekiel 16:4-5)

I retold for my audience the haunting opening scene from Amy Tan's *The Joy Luck Club*, in which a desperate Chinese mother leaves her twin infants at the base of a tree and walks away.

I passed by you, and saw you flailing about in your blood. As you lay in your blood, I said to you, "Live! and grow up like a plant of the field." (Ezekiel 16:6-7)

In a wonderful twist, a gracious adoptive Parent discovers the abandoned infant.

You grew up and became tall and arrived at full womanhood; your breasts were formed, and your hair had grown; yet you were naked and bare. (Ezekiel 16:7)

I felt red-faced when I read this part aloud. As the words came out of my mouth, I was wishing I had worn a looser shirt. And that I was shorter. And that I didn't have such long, beautiful hair.

I passed by you again and looked on you; you were at the age for love. I spread the edge of my cloak over you, and covered your nakedness: I pledged myself to you and entered into a covenant with you, says the Lord GOD, and you became mine. (Ezekiel 16:8)

Mine. The word touched my very core. I dared to hope that listeners who hadn't had the fortune of being forsaken would still understand how monumental and fantastic God's noticing and caring and choosing was.

This is the point in the story at which the biblical metaphor for God morphs from parent to lover. Though it's a little sudden, the change in relationship does seem to be the pattern into which we're invited by God as we move from immaturity to maturity.

> Then I bathed you with water and washed off the blood from you, and anointed you with oil. I clothed you with embroidered cloth and with sandals of fine leather; I bound you in fine linen and covered you with rich fabric. (Ezekiel 16:9-10)

The Lord does all that stuff her own parents wouldn't do. Our protagonist has been transformed from beloved child into beloved adult as God dresses her up like the radiant bride she is becoming.

> I adorned you with ornaments: I put bracelets on your arms, a chain on your neck, a ring on your nose, earrings in your ears, and a beautiful crown upon your head. (Ezekiel 16:11-12)

As the preaching class video camera rolled, I was reading this portion of the passage when one of the huge gold earrings I was wearing fell out of my ear. As it plummeted toward the pulpit, I stuck out my hand with a lightning quick reflex and caught that shiny thing. Altogether dignified, I simply continued on, looking like an odd liturgical pirate. Suffice it to say that since then, I have never worn large chunky earrings while leading worship. I have, however, quietly slipped this text to teenage girls trying to convince their mothers to let them get their noses pierced.

> You were adorned with gold and silver, while your clothing was of fine linen, rich fabric, and embroidered cloth. You had choice flour and honey and oil for food. You grew exceedingly beautiful, fit to be a queen. Your fame spread among the nations on account of your beauty, for it was perfect because of my splendor that I had bestowed on you, says the Lord God. (Ezekiel 16:13-14)

The beloved was beautiful because of *whose* she was. After this fourteenth verse, though, it's all downhill for Jerusalem. So I just stopped there. And while I was mostly taken by the cool fabrics and the nose ring, that other bit—the part about the kid abandoned in the field—was slowly taking root in my heart as well.

- six -

ONE WILY EMOTION CHIP

During seminary orientation I had noticed a tall, dark, handsome and apparently fun-loving guy galloping across the grassy quad of campus with a small woman on his back. No sooner had that cool drink of water caught my attention than I rebuked myself for being so superficial. Personal policy. These weren't the qualities, I reminded myself, that one ought to look for in another person. Especially one to whom I've never actually spoken. Been there, done that.

A few days later, that cute guy stopped me in the cafeteria to introduce himself as Peter. When he tapped my shoulder, I was still trying to act very sophisticated about not being drawn to him simply because of his looks. Thankfully, my personal policy included a friendship escape clause. I had every intention of finding out what *was* inside the incredibly fine packaging.

Peter and I quickly became friends. He had studied architecture at Clemson University and then worked a year stapling papers for a pharmaceutical company before coming to seminary. His was about as logical as the path I'd been traveling. Over the semester Peter and I continued to hang out. Although it was entirely obvious to me that we were meant to spend the rest of our lives together, he was not letting on.

Before Christmas break I finally initiated the dreaded relationship talk. Like everything else in my life, I felt conflicted about doing so. My new feminist friends encouraged me to do it, and my old not-feminist friends warned against it. I gathered up my courage and decided to talk to him. During that conversation, Peter confirmed that he just wanted to be friends.

I took it relatively well. Like any romantic psychotic worth her salt, I remained unconvinced he did *not* love me madly. If I had been rejected, I wasn't about to face it.

I had already arranged to spend the night at Peter's mother's house in North Carolina on my way to ring in the New Year with friends in South Carolina. That evening, Peter was off tinkering on some home repair project while I sat in the living room and chatted with his mom. In a seemingly off-handed comment, she remarked, "Peter says he doesn't want to date anyone up at school. How about you? Are you dating anyone?"

Picture deer caught in proverbial headlights.

"Nope," I replied, stunned. "Not dating anyone. Not me. No way. No sirree bob." It was the first time I'd said the word *Bob* out loud, without spelling it, in five years.

Was she messing with me? I hoped she was as oblivious as she seemed.

The fact that Peter had made it clear that we were "just friends" did nothing to prevent me from living in my own galaxy of delusion. At his mom's church on Sunday morning, I practiced sitting next to Peter in a pew as I suspected we might do together for the next six or seven decades. (I overlooked the fact that, since we were both in seminary, at least one of us would probably have to sit at the front of the sanctuary, high and lifted up, on some sort of liturgical throne.) Because my family no longer lived in my Illinois hometown, I secretly suspected I might actually get married to Peter in that very church one day. Thus, the galaxy of delusion.

When we returned to school, our friendship continued as normal. It was not until the second and final relationship talk, as the school year drew to a close, that I was finally able to truly hear those two horrible words reiterated from Peter's lips: "just friends."

Although I heard them, comprehended them and even accepted them this time, I protected myself from the full weight of their sting. Unlike my fathers, I reminded myself, Peter had no binding obligation to choose me. Disappointed but not devastated, I added Peter's name behind Max's onto the growing list of people who didn't realize what they were missing by not choosing me.

Not the Man for Me

By May I was looking forward to beginning my summer field-education placement at Westminster Presbyterian Church in Camden, New Jersey. The church was located just a few blocks from Urban Promise, formerly known as the Evangelical Association for the Promotion of Education.

My housemates, Kendra and Ellen, who I'd known in Camden before seminary, had followed the unfolding Peter saga since its inception. That summer the two bore witness to my sincere declaration that the romantic nothing I had shared with Peter was, in fact, over.

Our friendship, apparently, was not. Peter's first phone call that summer took me by surprise. I must have been tie-dying my diapers when the other infants were achieving object permanence, because I was always surprised that people remembered me when I was out of their sight.

I was cordial on the phone as we chatted about what was happening in the church he was serving in rural Georgia and what I was doing in Camden. Our conversation ended abruptly, however, when he had to hang up suddenly. He explained it was stormy outside, and he was afraid that he would get hit by lightning through the phone.

Left with the dull buzz of a dead line, my resolve only strengthened as I dropped the receiver into its cradle. "Well, ladies," I announced to Kendra and Ellen, "That settles it! Here I am, risking my life on dangerous city streets, and this poor guy can't even talk on the phone in the rain. Whew! I really dodged a bullet with this one, huh?"

Dutifully, they nodded in agreement. But I knew they were still thinking about what a hottie he was.

Peter called again a few weeks later. He wanted me to know that the women at the church he was serving were praying for me. I was, quite frankly, surprised. For a second I thought they might be praying for the woman who would one day be the wife of their beloved pastoral intern. Old habits die hard. Then I realized they were praying because I was living and working in the most dangerous city in America. What surprised me most was that I was good with that.

We talked for awhile and eventually got around to discussing our imminent return to campus. Peter was facing an agonizing personal decision. He wanted to bring his canoe back to school, and he had gotten his knickers all in a twist about whether or not he needed to purchase canoe liability insurance.

Canoe liability insurance. That's all I'm saying.

When we hung up I bellowed to Kendra and Ellen, and to the heavens, "How much more clear could it be that this is not the man for me?!?"

It felt really good to say it.

It felt right.

T.G.I.F. Carrot Cake

After a few weeks back at school, Peter and I were driving home from the nearby church that Scott was pastoring.

"Umm," Peter began awkwardly, "I was wondering if you wanted to go to T.G.I. Friday's sometime. I heard they have good carrot cake." Real smooth. A few nights earlier we had gone out to a diner with a group of friends, and I had mentioned that Friday's has the world's best carrot cake. Other than my mom's.

I was 82 percent sure he had just asked me out on a date. When I'd sworn off Peter in April, a bumbling yet sincere attempt at obedience, I'd done it in an Abraham-placing-Isaac-on-the-altar sort of way. If God had it in mind to yank Peter off the altar, who was I to argue? When he showed up Tuesday night and told me I looked nice, in my flowing peasant dress and Doc Marten boots, I knew it was a date.

As we lingered over our carrot cake, Peter spit out some blather about realizing over the summer how much he had missed me and that he would like for us to date. Feeling nervous and confused, I agreed.

Then he got a little more flustered and bumbled, "So what do we do *now?* Wanna get married?" I just laughed nervously. When Peter realized that had been sort of a weird thing to say on a first date, he laughed too.

Back on campus that evening, Peter came to my room to hang out as he had done so many times before. This time, though, was different. He kept *looking* at me. When I say *look*, I mean that his eyes were fixed on mine. It would have been like something in a romance novel, I suppose, if it hadn't made me so horribly uncomfortable. I felt absolutely unworthy of being the object of someone's full attention and adoration.

Wanting to appear less messed up than I was, I willed myself to look back into his beautiful eyes as long as I could. When I couldn't stand it any longer, I looked away and giggled. Because we were both feeling pretty giddy, my social incompetence was mostly disguised. From Peter.

But I knew. I knew that his steadfast gaze had exposed vulnerability in me. I couldn't *not* look away. I would later learn that the word for what I was experiencing was *shame*.

The next morning I called my mom to give her the scoop. Because she'd been tracking along with my latest seemingly ill-fated crush, she was delighted for me. And probably more than a little relieved to know I wasn't actually a deranged stalker. After I yammered about all the details of the evening, the first words out of her mouth were, "Do you need to go shopping?" Unfortunately, what I heard her saying was that I might want to improve my appearance to *keep* that fine man. I was a little irritated when we hung up.

I called my grandmother and gave her the same story. She immediately asked, "Do you need to go shopping?"

Irked, I told her in no uncertain terms, and with a very loud voice, exactly the same thing I had told her daughter: "I *got* him with these clothes, and I'll *keep* him with these clothes!"

I would later learn that the brilliant orange muumuu jacket, electric orange tennis shoes and tie-dyed purple jeans were among the first things that Peter had noticed about me. It would have been pretty hard not to. He actually liked them, though, which was not at all a given.

Peter had seen and accepted me for exactly who I was. It looked as if my days of crazy, desperate, greeting-card assaults, and of bellowing my undying love to someone just trying to help me look less ridiculous, were over. It seemed as if being in relationship with Peter might satisfy that deep hunger I had to be seen, heard and accepted.

Whether or not it would remained to be seen.

Every Woman's Dream Twig-Ring

To make a long story medium-length, Peter and I dated for a year before he proposed on our first date-iversary. He took me to Philadelphia, which looks out over Camden's skyline. Falling to his knee by the Delaware River, he proposed with a wooden decoy ring.

That's right, a decoy ring.

I could only assume he had taken to heart my insistent protests that I didn't want him to waste a lot of money on some fancy ring. What he actually offered me looked like the brambly twigs that are left over when all the grapes on the bunch have been eaten. Before I was really able to process the fact that the man with whom I wanted to spend the rest of my life had just given me produce scraps as the symbol of his undying affection, I agreed.

No sooner had I said yes than Peter was dragging me away from river's edge. He wanted to be a comfortable distance from the water so that when he untaped the container holding the *real* engagement ring, it wouldn't fall in. Naturally, he didn't want that ring to accidentally spring out of its container, fly through the air, bounce off the pavement, roll down the embankment, sink into the water and burrow in the slimy riverbed. That probably happens all the time.

I couldn't wait to tell my mom, who was in town and staying at Scott's. I drove over for breakfast the next morning just to see if she would notice my ring. Unfortunately, she was looking out the window as I floated toward the front door and caught me looking down at my hand to admire that shiny, sparkly thing. She knew darn good and well that I had never, ever, once peeked to check my personal appearance before. My secret was out.

Telling my friends was a whole other barrel of monkeys. I already knew that some feminists on campus equated an engagement ring with those hot poker things used to brand cattle. It signified that I was now someone's property. I dreaded telling them I planned to take Peter's last name as my married name. When I called Geni to tell her my great news, though, I did explain that I planned to use Peter's last name and go by Margot Starbuck Hausmann. Even I knew that's what old grand-mas did. Geni, though, still seemed a little taken aback that I was keeping Starbuck as my middle name. Teasing me about the biblical mandate for wives to submit to their husbands, she playfully chided, "You've gotta learn to submit, girl!" She was teasing, but she sort of meant it.

I couldn't win.

Wedding Season

Peter and I planned our wedding for graduation weekend. Although the bride often bears the brunt of the planning, Peter was much more in-vested in all the rigmarole than I was. On Sunday mornings I would catch him glancing up at the rafters of Scott's church while scribbling a diagram in his worship bulletin for Terry, who had graciously offered to arrange our flowers and create a lush garland for the rafters. Peter also chose the plodding, theologically correct hymns for our ceremony, in order to counterbalance my jive-rocking gospel choruses that a friend from Camden had agreed to play on the piano. Gripping the scanning gun to register us for gifts, he even led the death march through Macy's crystal and china section. Honestly, just hearing words like *stemware* and *tureen* made me feel sick to my stomach. Peter, on the other hand, who years earlier had picked out the china pattern he would one day own, was like a kid in a candy shop. Although I would have rather worn itchy monogrammed sweaters than own fine china, our relationship weathered the engagement.

The hard parts of the wedding planning season didn't have to do with being a full-time student, writing a thesis, working part time, teaching one of my amazing ring bearers—my one-year-old nephew Teague—to walk down the aisle with Isaiah, managing my most recent ill-fated small business venture or even helping Peter plan the wedding. Those were the easy parts. The hard parts, as with so many weddings, had to do with family.

Knowing Max would not respond, let alone show up, I had not invited him.

Though I phoned to tell Mel, my first stepfather, he chose not to attend.

Pam *would* attend, meeting my adoptive parents for the first time. No pressure there.

What felt particularly unwieldy was the issue of how Peter and I, still students, would pay for the wedding. Although nothing about the event was extravagant, it started to add up. We scrimped and saved anywhere we could. Scott was covering the costs at the church. His wife lent me her wedding dress. For my tender feet, I adorned twenty-dollar, white Converse Chucks with lace and pearls, tying them with elegant satin ribbon. To the dismay of our Italian New Jersey friends, we would forego a feast and serve our guests only cake and punch. (They have since forgiven us.) The morning of the wedding, Peter was still cutting lilies of the valley from a friend's yard and climbing tall ladders to remove ivy from their home for the great garland. To eliminate the cost of a DJ, I made a cassette tape of music that our reception guests could dance to and that was piped through a small speaker. Trust me: it was no cooler to host a party to a cassette tape back in the day than it would be today.

Months earlier, my dad had asked me point-blank what he should do for the wedding. I actually told him that he could fund the carrot wedding cake that we would order from a grocery store. I didn't even try to sweeten the deal with some fruity punch. He did exactly what I asked. I suspect he would have done anything I asked, but I asked small because I felt small.

Traditionally, a woman's wedding is the time that her worth is displayed for the community. The fact that I was an enlightened, modern woman wouldn't erase the significance of the event. Although I longed to be given away as *someone's*, no one claimed me.

One Wily Emotion Chip

As anyone knows, the fair maiden who has triumphed over adversity to win the prince's heart is supposed to live happily ever after. Fade to black, roll credits. The summer we were married, we moved to northern New Jersey, where Peter had taken a position as an associate pastor, and I naturally assumed that our life together would be a continuation of the happily-before I'd enjoyed thus far. Come to find out, really not so much. Instead, matrimony started a whole other chapter I never even saw coming.

It began with the unwelcome feelings. In one *Star Trek: The Next Generation* movie, the lovably impassive robot, Data, is reprogrammed with an "emotion chip." Suddenly the droid that was once without feelings becomes saddled with the human complications of fear, lust, anger, sadness and joy. The poor guy just goes haywire. During those first months of marriage, I began to suspect that at some moment during the wedding ceremony—perhaps while I was distracted by my cute ring bearers—someone had surreptitiously installed an emotion chip in lovably impassive me. Against my will, as if someone had flipped a CRAZY switch in my head, marriage became the volatile mad-scientist laboratory for all my new, unwieldy emotions.

On a typical weeknight, I would prepare dinner. (For the record, that sentence deserves all kinds of disclaimers about me having neither the inclination nor gifting to be a traditional Betty Crocker wife. Yet if every one of them were written down, the world itself could not contain the books that would be written. I will simply say here that because Peter was employed full time, and I was working part time, the lot of slopping some food onto a pair of plates at the end of the day had fallen to me.)

As Peter and I are both clockwork eaters, we had agreed that six o'clock would be our dinnertime. As the hour approached, I would glance regularly toward the grey ceramic wall clock as the long hand climbed upward. I'd slide two plates of hot food onto the table at six sharp, confident Peter would glide in as I finished filling the water glasses.

At six, though, sometimes there would be no Peter. My internal search engine would begin whirring, scanning for possible reasons that Peter had not arrived home as expected. Maybe he was driving someone in crisis to the hospital and had gotten stuck in traffic. There was always the glamorous Hollywood possibility that Peter been hit by a train or bus, but my anxiety really wasn't about his personal safety as much as it was about me being left alone.

This is so stupid, I would tell myself. *I am not this woman.* I am not the woman who is easily slighted or offended. I'm not the one who cries at the drop of a hat. I am *certainly* not the woman who comes unglued because her husband is late getting home from work. *That* woman is most certainly of the stripe that went to college to get her MRS degree. I am not she.

With each minute that passed, I would become more and more certain that the reason for Peter's unexplained absence lay with me. Had he told me he was going to the gym? Had I forgotten about a dinner meeting? Was there a presbytery meeting I should have been at too? At a strictly cerebral level, all of these were possibilities.

By eleven minutes after the hour, I would become exhausted from the work of trying to remember what I might have forgotten. My heart would race, and a dull, throbbing sadness would fill the front part of my head, pressing against the back of my eyes. A growing ache would pour through my chest and into my arms, a tingling that radiated from my achy chest all the way to the tips of all ten fingers, rendering my arms useless.

By 6:13, the voice in my head would take a turn for the sinister. The accuser would no longer be pointing fingers at me for overlooking a scheduling irregularity. Now a voice from deep within would rise up from the bowels of my own little hell to hiss, "Of course. Of course he's not here. Did you really think that you were worth showing up for?" That was the gist of it, but it was usually just the two words, "Of course." It only took two because I knew what they meant.

At seventeen minutes after six, my conscientious, trustworthy husband would rush in the door to find me slumped against a wall, half-comatose. Both of us knew that this was not the woman who had walked down the aisle three months earlier. That wily emotion chip was getting on my last nerve. Had I been able to locate it, I would have amputated just about any body part to get rid of it.

On top of the unwelcome feelings were the inappropriate thoughts. In those first few months I sometimes found myself thinking, *If something terrible happened to Peter, like an unfortunate collision while racing someone to the hospital, or falling onto a pointy shard of china, and I lost him right now, I'd be fine.* Somehow I knew that I wouldn't be like these other young brides on whom untimely misfortune falls, the ones who cry and feel sad. My reasoning was that since we hadn't shared a very long happily-ever-after, I'd probably be all right. Should tragedy strike.

I was wary about forming attachments. After all, the only people who are truly obligated to be there for you in this life are parents and spouses. On both counts, it's their *job*. These are the ones who are supposed to be there for you through thick and thin. The whole marriage shtick about "leaving and cleaving" just means that someone new has been hired to do the showing-up-through-thick-and-thin job. On the evening of May 20, 1995, in a little church in Hopewell, New Jersey, the assignment had fallen to Peter. For better or for worse, he had become my trust person.

I knew in my bones how dangerous attachments could be. When they ended poorly, which they usually did, I had always been the triumphant survivor. I was the girl who smiled and impressed everyone with how well adjusted I was; my first-grade teacher will still vouch for this.

Though on the surface I looked like any radiant bride, in my bones I was waiting for the relationship to end. I didn't know *how* it would end, but in my gut I knew that it would. Because my new groom didn't seem like the type to leave me high and dry—although really, which ones do?— I'd made up the stuff about the tragic mishaps. As any therapeutic professional might have guessed, my insides were more than a little anxious about attaching to Peter. As for the leaving and cleaving, I had the part about leaving my family down pat. I was actually a brilliant separation savant. It was the cleaving that was throwing a wrench into the works.

For the record, no one ever told me all this psychological stuff. I learned it the hard way.

We learned it the hard way.

Hallmark Holidays

The dynamics of my unwieldy internal life, both what I believed and what I desperately *wanted* to believe, were not entirely absent from my professional life. I doubt this would even be possible. Serving part time as an interim pastor at a nearby church provided my first opportunity to preach on the Sunday that fell on Father's Day. After all the angst around the F-word in seminary, I was feeling itchy to deliver a sermon that would set the record straight once and for all about the Father's goodness—for the 127 people who were listening to me, anyway. I did not take the responsibility lightly at all.

For that same record, I am keenly aware that celebrating the Hallmark holidays in the sanctuary can be dangerous business. I typically do not make it a personal practice. No one struggling with infertility needs all the mothers in the congregation to wear a flower on Mother's Day; for that matter, a lot of the silent birth mothers aren't so thrilled about it either. Don't even get me started on the Fourth of July.

Still, I felt compelled to say *something*. The whole father thing was the elephant in the sanctuary. Every week we prayed, "Our Father, who art in heaven." Every single person, even those who weren't quick-tongued enough to jump in on the first two words, had had some experience, good or bad, of a human father. Or fathers. Although their silent associations between a heavenly Father and a human one might lie dormant for fifty-one weeks a year, it became harder to dodge those elephant droppings on Father's Day.

The gist of the sermon was that though God is the one from whom human fatherhood *should* derive its essence, human beings do, by definition, fall short. If you want to know what Father is supposed to be, look at Jesus' dad. I just needed people to hear that. I needed *me* to hear that.

As worshipers left the sanctuary I received the usual comments about the service and my pretty hair. One woman in her early seventies grabbed my hands. Her eyes were wet. "I can't thank you enough," she choked out. "I've needed to hear that for a long time."

Just as I was feeling pretty great about that heartwarming encounter, another woman, who apparently didn't need to hear it, came through the line. She, too, let me know it.

As grinning worshipers continued to file by, I searched for the cause of the woman's resistance. Perhaps she was disenchanted with the rigid, systematic patriarchy running rampant throughout the Old Testament. If that was the problem, I couldn't do much about it. Maybe she, or someone she loved, had had an insurmountably bad experience with a horrible human father. If that was it, then I still desperately wanted to convince her that God is in the business of redeeming just such atrocities. My head was certain of it.

Wise Saul Man

During this time I also served part time as director of spiritual development at a local agency for individuals living with various physical and
developmental disabilities. As with the seniors in Santa Barbara, I was
able to relax into relationship with these new friends with the unspoken
assurance that they were not likely to leave me. Though the challenges
with which they lived were less easily disguised than mine, I was keenly
aware that I was no less broken. My job was to proclaim the liberating
truth that every individual is a beloved child of God. Since the staff and
families were already convinced that the residents were entirely worthy
of love and respect, it was a little like preaching to the choir. And, of
course, preaching to the preacher.

In the 1990s, the state had closed down its largest residential institutions in order to integrate the individuals served into the life of the
larger community. The agency for which I worked was one of the agen-
cies to welcome these individuals.

A resident who had lived in one of the large state institutions was
Saul, a Jewish man in his late forties. His face, far less worn than his
peers' in the community, sparkled with beautiful blue eyes and a radiant
smile. To be in Saul's presence was a joy. To my medically untrained eye,
Saul appeared completely paralyzed, and was required by his frail frame
to be in a reclining position whether awake or asleep. Although Saul was
a very social man, he was only able to verbalize a few words. His primary means of communication were blinking those beautiful eyes.

Despite the indignity of being transported to us by ambulance and
being dropped off at his group home with few personal belongings and
a large stack of medical records, Saul quickly won the hearts of our staff.
These devoted aides had been able to glean, from his previous caregivers, a little of Saul's story. For much of his life, Saul had been cared for
by his parents in their home. When his mother died and Saul's care be-

came too physically burdensome for his elderly father to manage, Saul was placed in the state institution. He lived there until he came to us, and the father who loved Saul continued to visit him there faithfully.

The next part is a little fuzzy. I imagine that the grown-up version of the telephone game that eventually brought it to my ears—one staff member whispering Saul's story to the next—had skewed its accuracy. The way I heard it is that when his father died, Saul was never told the real story. With the best of intentions, perhaps, Saul was "spared" the pain of his father's death. Saul was told simply that his father had gone out, on an errand, perhaps to the store, and that he would return later. I guess they thought Saul would buy it.

Years after the loss of his father, Saul's deep grief could be easily triggered by an event like a birthday or Father's Day. Sometimes Saul would begin to weep and moan with no evident explanation at all. Although he lived with mental and physical limitations, Saul was no different than any other man who had lost his father. And his mother. And his home. His community. The next home. His caregivers. Saul had lost every relationship he had ever known. When that sad place inside of him was activated, Saul would cry and bellow, "Da'y go way. Da'y go way! *Da'y go way!*"

My daddy has gone away.

Saul had, in his body, endured the loss of his father. Those around Saul wanted to believe that he couldn't grasp or didn't need to be troubled with the truth. Yet the human body, even one with bones as fragile as Saul's, holds a deep knowledge of presence and absence.

Classic Greek thought divided the human person into body, mind and spirit. But ancient Hebrew wisdom, as evidenced in Scripture, used just one word, *levav* לבב, to indicate a single heart-mind. There was no split. No division. No Greek categories attempting to control and manipulate what simply was.

Saul was more Jewish than anyone gave him credit for. I suspect we all are.

Encounters with Saul made me wonder if I still held, in my adult bones, the memory of losing my trust person as an infant. The fact that the loss was preverbal and preconscious did not seem to minimize its impact. And the fact that I couldn't rewind a mental film reel of the moment and play it back for a husband or pastor or therapist did nothing to lessen its sting.

On Plantar Fasciitis

All the standing involved with preaching, visiting folks in the hospital and leading worship as part of my chaplaincy work had been hard on my feet. I knew I needed help once I began greedily eyeing some of the nighttime orthotic devices used by the residents of the home where I worked.

I had read enough about chronic plantar fasciitis to understand what was happening down there. Because the damaged connective tissue running along the bottom of my foot had never been sufficiently treated, it had grown brittle and tight, like a rubber band from 1914 that you'd find in the attic. Every night as I slept those bands would contract, causing my foot to tighten up. Then when I stood up in the morning, the little fibers that had begun to reattach to my heel and forefoot during the night, having lost their elasticity, would start to tear away again.

How fitting. A painful and seemingly endless cycle of attaching and tearing away, which my heart had refused to feel, had found unauthorized expression in my feet.

The last semester of seminary, just before Peter and I got married, I had visited a podiatrist. In taking a few x-rays, he discovered that I had a needle in my toe. You may be thinking that "needle" is a medical term with which you are unfamiliar. It is not. It was literally a sewing needle—the pointy tip of one, anyway. Once the doctor mentioned it, I conjured up a vague recollection of stepping on a needle while in the manic throws of launching Starstruck Creative Clothing. I remembered finding a piece of needle in the blue plush carpet of the room I shared with Terry. Now, at long last, I knew where the other piece had landed.

The needle situation was completely unrelated to the chronic pain in my feet. My podiatrist wanted to remove it, though, so that it didn't drift away through the bloodstream and puncture a heart or a spleen. Nobody wants that. Because I would have to be off my feet for awhile after the procedure, we had decided to do it after the wedding. While many friends and family found it hard to fathom that I had been walking around on a needle for four years, by that time nothing could have been more unsurprising to me than learning that I had been living with a sharp metal object in my body and feeling no pain.

The needle wasn't the only foreign object that I ended up carrying around in my body during my twenties. A few years after Peter and I married, I became pregnant. As the weight gain of pregnancy increased the load my feet had to bear, I became unable to tolerate the pain. Already unable to walk to the bathroom in the middle of the night and forced to crawl, I knew I'd have to do the same thing to get to a baby's nursery.

My life had already become a revolving clinic door of visits to practitioners I hoped would help me. One podiatrist had suggested over-the-counter orthotics, which I bought and used. The spine and sports medicine doc had suggested anti-inflammatory medication and the use of a stretching apparatus, both of which I bought and used. A renowned sports medicine guru in the Midwest had suggested both the coveted night splints and a particular custom orthotic made from hard molded plastic.

My grandmother insisted on giving me the money to buy supportive

footwear even though it meant wearing ugly, lace-up man-shoes. If that's
not love, I don't know what is. Pam footed the bill for me to visit a respected orthopedist in New York City. He took one look at the hard orthotics in my man-shoes and announced with certainty that it was only
soft, squishy orthotics that would do the trick.

Before I reached his receptionist, I was in tears. Did I mention that
I'm not a woman who easily dissolves into tears? Let's be very clear on
that. This became the pattern for each new doctor's visit. Sometimes I
could make it all the way to the parking lot before I fell to pieces, but by
the time we got to squishy orthotics, I was entirely spent. I did not buy
them and I did not use them.

Just before I became pregnant, I decided that I was pretty much done
with feet doctors. Peter named the growing pile of therapeutic parapher-
nalia in our basement "the foot graveyard." It was. Stretching devices,
massagers and splints lay lifeless like dead bones. I had lost all hope that
the brittle sinews connecting mine would ever be brought back to life.

Zoë Lou

Peter and I welcomed Zoë Louise Hausmann into the world on February
19, 1999. I delivered her wearing supportive hiking boots. Nurses passing by in the hallway, on seeing those big feet sticking out over the end
of the bed, probably assumed they belonged to a lazy father stretched
out on his wife's clean sheets. One nurse actually rounded the corner
prepared to chew out some man and found me instead. She nicknamed
me "Miss Boots."

Holding our precious daughter to my breast, I marveled that she and
I were blood. Gazing up at me, her large eyes searched the face that
would, more than any other, reflect her inherent worth. I purposed that
she would see in my eyes and hear from my lips the truth of her inesti-
mable value.

After the nurses had swaddled Zoë and laid her in the open-face toaster oven, I watched as Peter's hulking silhouette loomed over her. Bending to place his large features inches from her miniature ones, the two soaked in one another. He couldn't take his eyes off of her. Shameless, she held his gaze.

Then, after she had been poked and prodded, Peter and I took turns photographing one another holding our daughter and then asked a nurse to snap one of the three of us. The earliest photo of me is a fading one from my foster home that Pam's social worker had surreptitiously slipped to her. The next was taken when I was three weeks old, held in the arms of my proud adoptive mother. I now knew how she must have felt inside. I couldn't imagine how Pam must have been aching somewhere else at the same moment.

Zoë's birth elicited a deep knowledge of my own entry into the world. And what Zoë had done in her birth she would continue to do with each passing year of her life. The security that she would enjoy with Peter and me—as an infant, then a toddler and eventually a girl—would become the foil against which my own honest experience would gradually unfold.

You know how it is with newfangled technology. One day I was programmed with an emotion chip, and before I even figured out how it worked they had already come out with E-chip 2.0. That would be my Zoë.

The view from the curb was that we were the perfect family.

seven

LOOKING FOR LOVE
IN TOO MANY FACES

The joy of motherhood did little to alleviate the debilitating bouts of sadness that continued to be triggered within me. One morning, as I parked my car in the lot of a therapist I'd begun to see weekly, I opened my door to see an old pickup truck pulling into a parking space behind mine. The driver, a man of medium build, had shaggy hair and dark-rimmed glasses. It was obvious he hadn't troubled himself with any cumbersome fashion updates since the seventies. His countenance resembled the one I had seen in a few faded photographs. One I see in the mirror.

It's my birth father and he has come for me. The thought burst forth without warning. I still had only a pocketful of information about my birth father. Among the sparse bytes were these facts: several decades ago he drove an old Ford truck. He had shaggy hair. He had facial features something like my adult ones. These were, of course, not nearly enough to identify the truck driver. And although he had never come looking for me, apparently there was some part of me that hoped that this day it would be true.

It hadn't been true in college when, like Annie, I occasionally dared to wonder if some passing strangers might have been my birth parents coming for me at last. It hadn't been true three months earlier when a vehicle slowed to a crawl while passing me as I pushed Zoë's stroller briskly through our neighborhood. It hadn't been true any of the times I had noticed other shaggy-haired strangers who I wanted to believe were noticing me.

Why would it be true then, just as I was on my way into therapy?

Hope.

Because I wasn't *completely* delusional, I did wonder why he would be there. In my state. In my town.

"To find you," Hope insisted.

But why would he be in this parking lot? Why follow me to my nine o'clock appointment? Unauthorized, Hope leaped to the assumption that he was planning to surprise me in the presence of my therapist, who could be a helping witness. I found it very thoughtful that they had been conspiring. My heart rate quickened.

I climbed the office suite's outside staircase, pretending not to notice the truck man behind me on ground level. I didn't want to ruin his carefully orchestrated plan by making eye contact prematurely. Self-conscious, I straightened my posture and smoothed my dress. Glancing in the reflection of the door's glass, I decided that he'd caught me on a pretty good day. It was summertime and I loved my aqua dress, light hair, tan skin and bright orange Indian beaded purse. I felt like myself.

Inside the hallway I flipped on the light switch to let my therapist know I'd arrived. I sat down in the waiting room, keeping my eye on the door. So full of what was bubbling inside me, I didn't even pick up a trashy celebrity magazine. I waited. Hope actually expected the truck man to come into the waiting room at any second.

He never did.

Time brought me back to my senses. I calculated how old my father must have been. I guessed fifty-five; the man in the parking lot couldn't have been much more than forty. As reality slowly dawned, I could admit that I'd known the guy seemed a little too short. A little too young. A little too real.

In addition to the occasional deluded daytime fantasy, I dreamed about my birth father at night. The general theme of these unconscious intrusions was that I'd be walking along a crowded city street and he would see me, recognize me, embrace me, take me home like a stray puppy and get to know me. Day and night, my needy inner child was simply wreaking havoc. That girl was wearing me out.

On the evening of my parking-lot fantasy, I googled Max. He had a phone number. The fleeting idea of calling him entered my mind, but then I decided that it was too risky. I would probably hang up. It had always been one of my personal policies not to indicate in any way that I wanted him, that I might have needed him. A hang-up had "needy" written all over it. And although my imaginary profile of him wasn't tech-savvy enough to have caller ID, I was just wary enough to believe that he would still know it was me. And be disgusted.

While I was still googling, the door burst open and Peter came in. I quickly minimized the screen that revealed my dirty little secret.

I was ashamed that I wanted him so badly.

Gold Teeth, Loud Music and Bottomless Sadness

As part of my chaplaincy work, I was involved with a local clergy association that met monthly for lunch and discussion. At one meeting a couple of guys on staff at a local Pentecostal church shared that they'd been having some particularly vibrant worship services on Friday nights. These gatherings had actually been birthed while the senior pastor had been out of town. I knew immediately that had "good stuff" written all over it.

The pastors, humbly as surprised by this turn of events as anyone, described individuals in their congregation growing in their faith and even being healed emotionally and physically. Though they didn't bill that healing bit as the main attraction, it was definitely what caught my attention. Later, I even heard a rumor at my workplace that a few of the teeth in the mouth of one pastor's wife had turned into gold! Though intrigued, I just could not bring myself to ask my colleague whether or not any of his bride's body parts had been replaced by anything one might find on the periodic table. I tucked the information away, though, and made plans to visit that great church to get my feet healed.

Though I tried to sneak into the rollicking sanctuary unnoticed, Randy, an associate pastor, had an uncanny "newbie" radar. Though he was buried somewhere on the far side of the seven-hundred-seat sanctuary when I crept in, he instantly came to me to extend a hearty welcome and make a little too much small talk. So much for sneaking. Though I was an ordained Presbyterian pastor, I'm pretty sure that Randy still saw me as a seeker. This, of course, was not entirely untrue.

The worship music was spectacular. A twelve-member band led us in moving choruses that were occasionally accompanied by modestly costumed liturgical dancers waving fabulous shiny flags. As someone who regularly looked for any excuse to dance in church, I really *wanted* to be happy. I wanted to bounce and wiggle and wave. I wanted my hands to be free to go up or down as they saw fit. I was even willing to sing. What happened in me, though, was something else.

The music, much of which praised God as a trustworthy Father, elicited from deep within me a heavy sadness. Unlicensed tears poured down my cheeks. Through wet eyes I watched a sleeping baby nearby, held in her mother's arms. Her daddy was standing next to her mommy.

I thought of Zoë, at home with Peter, slumbering soundly in her crib. Besides the obvious miracle of a baby sleeping when the music was three thousand decibels, I was touched that that was where the baby's parents had taken her. More tears.

Since the opening worship songs took twice as long as an entire church service in our congregation, I had to slip out to use the bathroom about halfway through the spectacle. Turning to leave the sanctuary, I noticed a father sitting in the back row with his arm around his teenage son. The sight undid me. More tears and aching in my heart.

I put myself through this horrible ordeal on many Friday nights before I was able to recognize the pattern. I'd go to the church hoping that my feet would be healed. The Spirit, at work in the worship music, would completely undo me. Then, after the preaching, I'd humbly go forward for prayer, hoping to be slain—I mean really knocked out—in the Spirit.

I never was.

What happened instead was that I felt lots and lots and lots of sadness. Back at home, Peter, less an enemy of emotion than I am, suggested that maybe I just needed to get it all out. I told him in no uncertain terms that I thought that was really stupid. Didn't he realize that I could have moonlighted at that church every Friday night until the second coming and still not get all my sad out?

32 Pentecostal Flavors

If previously I had been a loose woman about going from doctor to doctor for help with my feet, I was even more of a floozy when it came to healing ministries.

A lot of people knew about my bad feet. I'd told almost everyone I met, mostly in righteous self-defense to explain the horrible man-shoes. A neighbor of ours was an Algerian Christian of the Pentecostal stripe. John believed that it was God's will for every Christian to be healed of everything, because what Father doesn't want to do that for his children? Although I wasn't entirely onboard theologically, when he put it that way it did sound pretty convincing. It was what I desperately wanted to believe.

The Sunday I attended John's Arabic-speaking church, I wore a headset so that I could hear an English translation of the pastor's words. It was actually more fun to listen to the Arabic. When it was time to go forward for healing, I dutifully processed. Gathering up all the faith I could, I willed myself to suppress any lingering doubts. When I reached the front John was next to me. I suddenly wished I'd thought to ask him for the Arabic translation of, "Do you know that I'm Presbyterian? You have no idea what you're dealing with here, buddy."

I didn't go down.

I had also met a couple of Roman Catholic Pentecostals at work. The great thing about all these charismatics was that they believed that God still *did* stuff! Like heal feet. And hearts. Just because the Anglo Jersey Pentecostals and the Algerian ones hadn't worked, who was to say that the Catholics wouldn't pull through for me?

My new friends invited me to a service of prayer and healing. What most affected me during that evening wasn't the homily or the singing (although, as usual, the worship music did do me in). What most captured my attention was the kind face of a man in his sixties. Peaceful, relaxed, he was seated across the aisle from where I sat. I stole glances at him when I thought he was praying or otherwise occupied. He just *looked* like he would be a gracious father. Perhaps he had come that evening to pray on behalf of one of his children. I imagined that he, sharing the same house and dinner table with them, would have been kind and interested, firm but gentle.

Glancing ahead in the bulletin, I knew I'd have an opportunity to touch him, grazing his palm, when the congregation shared the peace of

Christ. This was why I'd been trying to wipe my snot on my clothing instead of my hands. Everyone knows that's the polite thing to do. When it was at last time to exchange greetings of peace, I was already entirely undone by who I imagined he might be. As me and my drippy face moved from person to person, saying the holy words, I was keenly aware of this man's physical presence.I was starving for him and would not sit down until I'd had a taste.

Although I moved my mouth as I approached him, I don't think I even got all the syllables out. I tried to say, "The peace of Christ be with you," but I'm pretty sure that just a moany whine escaped. When I politely extended my hand, he surprised me by reaching his arms out to embrace me warmly. Warm enough to completely melt me.

Postal Fantasies

A few weeks later, after driving home from work and straight into the garage, I stepped outside into a drizzly rain to fetch the mail before going inside. As I did, I found myself fantasizing about the best possible thing I might find in that tin rectangle so full of possibility. Although I wished it weren't so, the best thing I could imagine would have been a letter from Max. Even though he had expressed no interest in me during the three years I'd spent in Princeton, I had still sent him a change-of-address card to let him know we had moved to North Jersey. I had no pride. My married name had also changed. None of these obstacles would have been hindrances if *I* was trying to find someone, but I realized that a guy who wasn't even trying needed all the help he could get.

Even having been given my new name and address, he never sent a letter.

Had my dreams come true, I would have discovered a damp, white envelope in the box. Both the return address and mine would have been handwritten. It would most certainly have borne an American flag stamp—with the desired DNA licked onto the back. Return address would have been Manhattan.

Dear Margot, it would begin. I'm sorry I haven't been able to be in touch. Please forgive me. I have thought of you often. A few years back I actually hired a detective to gather some more information about you. He sent a few photos and you look a lot like my sister.

I would not have even *minded* that he was a creepy stalker. Clearly, I craved it. It would continue,

Though my family never knew about you until recently, my mother and sister are now both anxious to meet you. I am too. I hope you have time for a brief visit. I'd love to hear more about your art and what's happening in your life.

It would most certainly be signed,

Yours, Max.

Mail had never really panned out for me the way I'd hoped it might.

Pam had always described Max as a great guy. From the time I had first located him, when I was twenty-two, she always thought that eventually he would come around and be willing to be in touch. For the first five years she had stayed out of the whole nothing between Max and me. If she pushed, Pam feared, he might pull away even further. I agreed it had been a good call. After five years, though, Pam realized there was no risk of driving him further away than he already was—which was, like, Jupiter. A finder after my own heart, she tracked him down in Maine— who knew?—and gave him a call.

When she reported the conversation to me later, I learned that she had actually said all the things that I thought he should know. I was a great young woman. He'd really like me. He should give me a call.

I knew that there would be no call.

The Greatest Thing

Ducking inside the house, pawing through the *real* stack of mail I had grabbed from our box, I recognized a return address with Seth's last name on it. It was from his parents in Illinois. Seth's mom, Penny, had sent me a pamphlet about an upcoming conference in Wheaton, Illinois, sponsored by Pastoral Care Ministries, a teaching and healing ministry. She attached a note offering me a bed in their home if I came. The invitation took me off guard. I dropped into a kitchen chair. Penny had no way of knowing that I had been wanting to attend one of these conferences since I'd read my first book by the ministry's founder, Leanne Payne, several years earlier. Since we weren't in the regular habit of corresponding, and since she didn't know about my injured feet, and since I'd never mentioned to anyone other than Peter that I wanted to go, the correspondence struck me as being possibly just a wee bit divinely inspired. Daring to believe that God could and would do some sort of miracle on my behalf, I decided to go.

Faster than you can cue up "Maybe God Is Tryin' to Tell You Somethin'" from *The Color Purple,* I had sent in my application and made flight arrangements. My mom, still in California, offered to fly east to care for Zoë while I was gone. With Peter working full time, we couldn't have pulled it off without her. Even though I knew my mom would have given her left lung to spend time with Zoë, her generous gesture on my behalf still touched me deeply.

When I arrived in Illinois, Seth's parents graciously welcomed me into their home. The conference began on Monday, June 12.

By day two, which happened to be my birthday, I was ready to go home.

On Tuesday, a speaker had told the story of a ruptured relationship he had endured as a very young child. Although for years he had never thought twice about its impact, he later realized that the episode had had a devastating and enduring effect on his sense of identity. Imagining precious, trusting Zoë toddling around at home, I wept. The tears, though, were not for her, secure with her daddy and grandmother. Instead, they were at last for me. The absence from Zoë had exposed my own grief. It was not exactly the soothing balm I'd been hoping for on my birthday.

Following the session, a trained counselor prayed with me and asked me to let God show us a picture of my heart. I silently thought that God should have told her that I had come to get my *feet* healed, not my heart. Nonetheless, closing my eyes, I immediately pictured a hard sphere with cracks in it. I got the sense that there was something soft in the middle, sort of like a Tootsie Pop. The woman with whom I was praying said that she was receiving some divine transmission (though not with those words). She was seeing my heart as something like the moon, with craters and cracks. Though it wasn't the kind of spiritual glamour shot a girl dreams of, it was most certainly true.

That's when I should have known I was in trouble. The Tootsie Pop television commercial from my childhood featured a boy asking a cow, a fox and an owl, "How many licks does it take to get to the Tootsie Roll center of a Tootsie Pop?" No one knew, because each one crunched it with their little animal teeth or beak before they reached the Tootsie Roll center. The smarty-pants owl started licking and counting, but only made it to three licks before biting a hunk out of it. At the end, after the narrator answered his own question, "The world may never know."

I was *sooo* Tootsie Pop. The lickin' I'd been taking felt interminable, and now it felt like I was being crunched up and spit out.

I returned to Seth's childhood home that night a complete mess, feeling the sting of my earliest birthday loss. I could have been a *Saturday*

Night Live sketch: the Emotionally Undone Houseguest. Had Seth been home we probably would have enacted and videotaped that very skit, which of course would have made me feel much better.

Seth's parents were very gentle with me. After we finished breakfast the next morning, his father invited Penny and me to stand, join hands and pray in the kitchen. The gracious gesture meant the world to me. I had received prayer ministry before from women, of course, but Seth's dad caring for me like that blew me away. It felt just as good as I'd always imagined it would.

Sweetest Little Baby in Town

Back at home, a friend named Emily also welcomed me into her home in order to pray for me. Though I had long ago given up trisecting the body of Christ, she was a "Holy Spirit" Christian if there ever was one. As I shared my story, she would "hmph" or "mmmm" at certain points. I could only assume she was receiving some sort of spiritual satellite signal. I'd covered the basics—adoption, alcoholism, divorce—and had even forayed into young adulthood and marriage when she suddenly interrupted me and began singing.

Hush little baby, don't say a word, Papa's gonna buy you a mockingbird . . .

It took me a few moments to process what I was hearing. I quickly reviewed in my mind what I'd shared with her up to that point. Why was Emily singing the lullaby that I remembered my father singing to me as a child? I'd mentioned nothing about it.

And if that mockingbird don't sing, Papa's gonna buy you a diamond ring.
If that diamond ring gets broke,
Papa's gonna buy you a billy goat . . .

Emily had been able to deduce—probably with regular human pow-
ers—that I was stinging from a few bad gifts. She sang that whole song
until at last she got to the end:

You'll still be the sweetest baby in town.

Though I trusted Emily, that's the part that felt like it was up for
grabs. I wanted to believe that I was the sweetest baby in town, that I
was worthy of good gifts, but if I was honest, it was pretty hard to swal-
low. Bad gifts = bad girl.

Emily did battle for me that day in prayer. When I left her home and
drove back to my own, I checked my body to see if I felt any of that
warm, Holy Spirit sensation I'd heard so much about from others.
Though I could not locate an identifiable tingle, something about my
body was different. Slowly, I realized what it was.

It was actually the absence of tingle. What was missing was a constant buzz zipping around through my bloodstream. If vigilance could
have been bottled up, poured into a syringe and shot into a vein, I most
certainly would have tested positive. Off the charts. But here's the crazy
thing: I never even knew I had it until that day. I had never noticed the
hum of that liquid defense until it was gone. That's what was different
about my body. Like a tiny, juicy gazelle dropped into a lion's den, I'd
been moving through life in a constant state of vigilance, waiting to fend
off the next threat. And although the vigilant tingle would soon return,
at least I had been given a taste of what life was like outside of the lion's
den.

Me And Oda Mae

Peter had been a prince about caring for our daughter during every doctor's appointment, every healing service, every conference, every home
visit and every therapy session. This was why I really wanted him to see

a profitable return on his investment. Understandably, he had begun to harbor concerns that I might just be an insatiable healing junkie. Though a man of strong faith, he was less convinced than I was that each new method or church or conference or therapy would hold the magical key to my redemption. This is why, when I returned from Illinois, I decided to prove to him that I was most certainly *not* addicted to healing. I'd show him.

Peter and I had driven to south Jersey, near Camden, and had enjoyed a great evening at the home of our friends Bruce and Pamela Main. When we finished dinner, Pamela curtly informed Peter and Bruce that the men-folk were responsible for cleanup and childcare while she and I retired to the den. I had no idea why this was the plan, but I liked it.

Once she had gotten me settled in comfortably on the couch, and had sealed the doors, Pamela invited me to pray with her. Of course, I was game. I was also secretly grateful that Peter had witnessed for himself that I had not even gone out looking to score that hit.

Picture Whoopi Goldberg as Oda Mae Brown in the movie *Ghost*, leading a fake séance. Even if you missed the movie, I think you can still imagine Whoopi Goldberg leading a fake séance. That's what it felt like. Pamela would start giggling, settle herself down a little and give me an instruction. A few minutes later she'd say, "No, no, that's not it," and she'd give me a different instruction. More giggling. Whoopi was just slightly more professional.

In the course of that effervescent therapy, Pamela invited me to let God show me a moment in my life. I immediately pictured the night that my parents gathered our family together to tell Scott and me they were getting divorced. It was a night in which I was completely void of emotion. That was the real-life scene, in my memory.

In the prayerful one, as Pamela and I invited Jesus to be present behind our heavy yellow door, I saw Jesus gently touching each one of us on the back with compassion—my mommy, my daddy, Scott and me. Then he came around the circle and picked me up. Jesus held me and experienced my sorrow with me. As he held me, Jesus helped me get my sad out. Girl-Margot wept and wept as Jesus held her in his arms. Jesus wept too.

I sat silently on Bruce and Pamela's couch, experiencing the sorrow that should have happened so long ago. Jesus bore it with me. Every once in awhile, the antsy part of me would prayerfully suggest to Jesus that he and I might be just about done with our prayerful crying. Each time, though, there was more. And more. And more. After a good long while, I had the sense that we'd done enough for one night. I also calculated that the dishes were probably finished.

I always wanted these healing sessions to fix everything up once and for all. The spiritual surgery to remove the hardened junk around my heart, I imagined, should be as simple as the painless buzz of the medical saw that is used to remove plaster casts from arms and legs. Instead, this prayer turned out to be one more emotional lickin'. That's not to say it didn't remove some shell; it most certainly did. I just thought that God should have poked around a little deeper in the divine toolbox to find that magic buzz saw.

Glimmer of Hope

Peter wasn't the only one wearying of each new healing possibility. I was, too.

One Sunday afternoon the pastor with whom Peter served, our dear friend L'Anni, invited me to go with her to pray for a friend experiencing back pain. After we prayed with Angela, I listened as she gushed on and on about her fabulous doctor. He was an osteopath, she explained—whatever that was. I was such a sucker that by the time we left Angela's house, I was sold. On a doctor who practiced in another state.

Thankfully, the state was New York. For my first appointment Peter and I pushed Zoë's stroller one block from our home in Pompton Lakes to the bus stop, rode the bus twenty miles into the city and walked a mile toward the doctor's office on Sixth Avenue. With some extra time before the appointment we visited the Guggenheim art museum, Zoë packed on Peter's back. One of the exhibits included a painting of a human foot whose fascia opened up to pour out human excrement. It was surreal on two counts.

In the doctor's waiting room, Zoë, liberated from her carrier, learned how to crawl. Daring to hope, I interpreted her emerging mobility as a promising sign. An assistant invited me into a treatment room and asked me lots of questions about my condition. When did it begin? How did it happen? Had there been other treatments? I hoped that the *real* doctor was going to read all that stuff before he saw me. I always wonder whether they do.

When the doctor ambled into the room, the first thing I noticed was that he limped a little. He looked like he lived with pain. I described to him my situation. I crawled to the bathroom in the middle of the night to avoid bearing weight. Every morning I experienced discomfort the moment my feet hit the floor. I wore sneakers in the shower to avoid the unforgiving porcelain tub. By the end of the day the pain was excruciating, often bringing me to tears. The next morning it would all begin again.

Doctor Lance's face crinkled with compassion, and he spoke gently. "This can be very painful," he said. "There are a number of different things we can try. We're going to work with this until we get you some relief." His words rolled over my heart like healing ointment.

My first impulse was to wonder whether or not he had children. Isn't that a funny thought? I thought he'd make a great dad. But that real moment, in the real New York City, was actually strikingly similar to the dreams I'd had about my birth father. Those were the ones in which I was seen and heard and known. Except, of course, my newest physician was not my birth father. Don't you know, though, I would have done any crazy thing that doctor told me to do? And that's exactly what I did.

Twice a week I made the cumbersome journey to Manhattan in order to pay lots of money for him to manipulate my feet and ankles and calves. I also went to physical therapy twice a week, closer to home. That's where I got to run on a treadmill in a large glass tank of water in the treatment room. And what woman doesn't want to jog in a bathing suit before a captive, bored audience of other people being poked and stretched?

I know exactly why I did that silly thing. There was someone who cared. I had been seen and heard and known. It's what I'd been after all along. The fact that most of the doctors I'd visited were about the age my birth father would have been at the time was not lost on me. I wanted for one of those doctors to see my pain, to listen to me and to care—even if that person couldn't fix me.

I know it sounds crazy to say that I wanted all of that more than I wanted to be healed physically, but it's true. I did.

Heaven Sent

As my feet grew worse, I couldn't imagine how my body would be able to walk for the additional five or six decades that I planned to live. I was at the end of my shoestring when I just laid it out on the line with God. "Since all of my ideas—which, for the record, have been creative, innovative and plentiful—have not seemed to be in the cards, why don't we do this your way."

Of course, as soon as I offered to relinquish control, I immediately continued to outline more possibilities for divine consideration. "You can lead me to the right doctor. You can give me a dream that provides the healing I'm after. You can point me in the direction of someone to whom you've given the gift of healing. You can give me some big idea. You can use Scripture to heal me. Let's just put the ole' medicine ball back in your court and see what you come up with."

That's when a little idea dropped out of heaven and right into my head. Although many doctors had recommended stretching every morning, the exercises usually served to make the pain *worse* throughout the day. These early morning stretches, when my feet were already so tight, were actually promoting the tearing that they were meant to prevent.

The great idea God planted in my noggin was that I would no longer begin the day with a rigorous, weight-bearing stretch. Instead, I would sit on the side of my bed and let my feet rest on the floor, bearing no weight, for ten minutes. That's right, the big idea was that I would sit on my behind. What this did for my feet, though, was allow them to gently flex from the nighttime state of contraction into a ninety-degree position before bearing weight. Then, when I did stand up to walk, my feet, ankles and calves were ready for the day.

If you're a lazybones, I know exactly what you're thinking: *that is the best exercise ever!* And it is. I've never missed a day since. There's no question in my mind that that big idea about quietly rooting myself each morning was heaven sent.

Getting Tom Sawyered

One day I was reading the second chapter of Exodus during my morning stretch. The Israelites, enslaved in Egypt, were in quite a pickle.

The Israelites groaned in their slavery and cried out, and their cry for help because of their slavery went up to God. God heard their groaning and he remembered his covenant with Abraham, with Isaac and with Jacob. So God looked on the Israelites and was concerned about them. (Exodus 2:23-25 NIV)

I wondered for a brief moment if I could have made that up. I checked again and, sure enough, there it was in black and white. God heard. God saw. God cared. It was exactly the thing for which my heart had been longing. I continued reading. Right after the author *tells* us this so-great-it's-hard-to-believe-it's-true thing about God, we are *shown* it when God speaks to Moses.

> *I have indeed seen the misery of my people in Egypt. I have heard them crying out because of their slave drivers, and I am concerned about their suffering. So I have come down to rescue them from the hand of the Egyptians and to bring them up out of that land into a good and spacious land, a land flowing with milk and honey—the home of the Canaanites, Hittites, Amorites, Perizzites, Hivites and Jebusites. (Exodus 3:7-8 NIV)*

God saw, God heard, God cared. I have to believe that at this point Moses was totally stoked. Big G was in da house! And not only was the God who was about to slip Moe his business card going to rescue the people he loved, he was going to give them a new home, a better home. God continues,

> *And now the cry of the Israelites has reached me, and I have seen the way the Egyptians are oppressing them. (Exodus 3:9 NIV)*

In case it wasn't clear already, God heard and God saw. Moses was now doing the running man in his bare feet—which, for the podiatric record, I highly discourage. Then God commands,

> *So now, go. I am sending you to Pharaoh to bring my people the Israelites out of Egypt. (Exodus 3:10 NIV)*

The dancing stops. Moe's brow furrows. His head tilts to the side as he asks, "Come again?"

With all due respect, do you see how God is a little bit like a crazy person here? In the same divine mouthful, God announces both that he has come down to rescue the Israelites and also that he is sending Moses to do the job. The sort-of-crazy part is that in God's mind there doesn't seem to be any discrepancy there. The fact that God is doing this thing, but we all really know that Moses had to do it, seems to make complete sense in God's madness.

This passage in Exodus confirmed to my heart that God cared. God not only cared about my physical suffering but also about the deep, hungry longing that I had to be seen, to be heard, to be known. It also convinced me that God was in the unlikely business of using human beings to do his bidding.

That's the part that left me feeling a little conflicted. On the one hand, I knew that I had been experiencing grace through human instruments like Emily, Pam Main, Seth's parents and Doctor Lance. On the other hand, I couldn't help but wonder whether God had also given the marching orders for the adults who had hurt me along the way.

I was not yet ready to admit it, but somewhere, in my bones, I suspected that God had.

- eight -

STRANDED IN
A SCORPION DESERT

"It's your flavor!" Peter's friends had gushed with delight.

Eighteen-year-old Peter was in Durham, North Carolina, to visit friends at Duke University. Raving about a local Presbyterian congregation, they gave glowing reports about the church's evangelical theology, intentional community life, heart for outreach and crazy, vibrant worship.

"Um . . ." Peter had hedged. "Are you sure? I think you might be confused."

They weren't. During his visit Peter, then a freshman at Clemson University, ducked into Blacknall Memorial Presbyterian Church and struck up a conversation, and then a friendship, with one of the pastors there, Allan.

Six years later, after we had begun dating, Peter brought me through Durham to meet him. Allan had been like a breath of fresh air to two drowning divinity students. Halfway through seminary, Peter and I both felt as if we were losing God-given parts of ourselves as we negotiated the path toward ordination. One night I dreamed I was suffocating, and the next night I saw my paints, notebook and Bible washed down a rapid stream. Peter and I were both exhausted by the conflicts, debates and theological declarations within the Presbyterian Church (USA) and on our campus. We hadn't given up on Jesus, per se, but the denomination was getting on our collective last nerve. Whiny and weary, we asked Allan, "How can you be so optimistic about the church?"

Deadpan, Allan asked us, "Have you ever *read* the Bible?" Allan loved the church because Jesus did. Through Scripture, he could see and hear and taste what Jesus' big plan was for the people who were called God's own children. Allan's vision of Jesus' vision sustained us through our final semesters of seminary.

Since Zoë's birth, Peter and I had been considering living closer to family. Peter's family was clumped in the Southeast. Mine was spread out in Washington, California, Arizona, Indiana, Rhode Island and Massachusetts. Aiming for his clump, Peter had begun to browse online in search of churches in North Carolina that were searching for pastors.

One day while Zoë napped, I was at home designing a fabulous line of inspirational "Walk with the Lord" greeting cards. The cards featured ink drawings of all my favorite comfortable shoes. I was painting a running sneaker when the phone rang. I picked it up to hear Peter, breathless, on the other end. He was calling from our church, across the street. He'd been looking at available positions and had learned that there was an opening for a copastor at Blacknall, in Durham. Fourteen minutes later he was licking the envelope of his application and plunking it in the mailbox.

What was scariest for this spousal humanoid was that we weren't at all dissatisfied in New Jersey. We had a great church, and we loved Peter's colleague in ministry there, our precious friend L'Anni. You know that fabled dog with a bone in his mouth that sees his reflection in a pond and opens up to grab the bigger bone? I didn't want to end up like that poor boneless guy. Peter, though, had an eerie sense—some would call faith—that the whole deal was in God's hands, whichever way it turned out. He would be content to go or to stay.

In the summer of 2001, Peter was called by the congregation of Blacknall Memorial Presbyterian Church, and we moved to Durham, North Carolina. There Peter would serve as copastor with Allan.

Abandoned

Blacknall Memorial Presbyterian Church is adjacent to Duke University. The congregation is somewhat transitional, with many students, faculty and staff arriving for orientation and leaving upon graduation or in pursuit of sabbatical refreshment. In order to build community among members, the women's ministry hosted dessert gatherings each autumn, by neighborhood, to give new women and established ones a chance to know one another. After we had lived there a year or two, I volunteered to coordinate one of these "zip code parties," assuming that it wouldn't be difficult to enlist about ten other women to pull it off.

True to my expectations, all ten women I asked were eager to serve. One or two had replied to my e-mail to let me know they couldn't make the planning meeting. One doctor on our team would be on call that night, so I knew she was iffy. This, in my mind, still left an acceptable quorum of seven or eight of us. The afternoon of our planning meeting I got a message from the hostess letting me know that if her family wasn't back from swimming by seven, we could just let ourselves in to her home and begin. Fair enough.

At 7:16 p.m. that evening, I was still waiting alone on her porch. Stinging memories, real and imagined, raced through my mind. I saw my birth father hurrying out of the hospital after my birth. I visualized my relinquishment days later, being handed over by my birth mother to a social worker. I remembered my parents' divorce, my father's leaving. I even pictured the empty living room where I waited alone the evening I threw the lame party during college. Each image confirmed my suspicion that not only was I unable to prevent others' absences, I was so flawed that I actually *caused* them. A familiar lying voice hissed, "There's something wrong with you. It's your fault people don't show up. You deserve this." Though I recognized the familiar pattern, I was unable to quell the anxiety, which mounted with each passing minute.

Longing to leave, I remained frozen in place, stuck on so many levels. I was still trying to please, as if my good behavior could hold the adults in my life in place, could secure them like Velcro. Though it had never worked before, I knew no other strategy. My body raced with a familiar, tingling ache running from the end of my fingertips, through one arm, across my chest, and back through the opposite arm, stinging both palms and each finger. My emotional Velcro, fuzzy from too many tear-aways, pulsed with anxious energy. The prickling sensation in my skin and bones, the horizontal stretch where *embrace* should have been, stung from the absence of any reciprocal hold from longed-for adults.

Even the wrong ones.

Eventually two women did show up. Both happened to be adoptive mothers. Biting my lower lip to hold in so much pain, I bravely tried to keep my overwhelming sadness under wraps. It spilled out anyway. Gathering me up as they would their own daughters, the two prayed for me.

As often as my emotions got the best of me like this, I longed for the good old days before my unwieldy emotion chip had been activated. When I went home that night, I actually tried to bring a few of them back.

Going Home

Having heard that Dave, a friend from high school, was performing at a comedy club in Chicago, I phoned Seth, Mindy and a few other old friends from around the country to talk them into meeting there for a weekend in the spring to catch the show. Because Dave's act was pretty much poking fun at a middle-aged couple who bore a striking resemblance to his parents, it felt an awful lot like what we really did in high school.

I flew to Chicago on a Friday. With several hours to spare before the show, I asked the limo driver, who had picked me up at O'Hare, to drop me off on the edge of my hometown so that I could stroll through the picturesque village.

Crunching fallen spring pods, I inhaled their fragrance. I never noticed the smell when I was growing up. How could I have? It was the air I breathed. Bending over, I reached down to pick one up. I was a little surprised, quite frankly, to see adult feet at the end of my legs.

Uninvited tears rushed down my cheeks. Believe me, I know that the "I-couldn't-believe-I-was-crying" bit is getting a little old. I was tired of it myself. Every time, however, I was truly taken by surprise. I didn't know if other people planned their cries, but my teary emotional ruptures always seemed to take me off-guard. Sniffing, I dragged the back of my hand across my face. Related to no memory in particular, yet somehow to all of them, I was overwhelmed by an anguished ache.

So much for the good old days.

Despite my bleary vision, I noticed the limo driver had looped back around on Park Boulevard for his return trip to the airport. I had just gushed to him about how excited I was to be visiting the town where I'd grown up; now, if he saw me, it would look like I had lied. I tried to look normal as he passed. I didn't want him to see me this way.

I didn't want to *be* this way.

After six blocks, I turned onto my street. Waiting for me on the corner was an absurdly appropriate front-yard scene. A neighbor's lawn, still holding small patches of winter's snow, displayed a disabled snowman family. Mother had lost a stick arm. Father's nose had fallen off. The kids, beginning to puddle, were shedding their clothes.

My gaze riveted on the warming daughter. I knew intuitively that the lass would not survive the season. My own fear—that the thawing of my frozen sadness might actually kill me—had taken cold, lumpy form.

I kept walking. Squinting past the branches of leafless spring trees, I could just make out the iron digits on our front door: 733. I wondered briefly if the present owners had ever molded a key for that abandoned lock. Each step I took toward the brick Tudor loosened the tap of this snow-girl's tears. Plodding mechanically, I became less and less aware of the neighbors' houses I was passing.

I tried to soothe myself with thoughts of all the good things had happened behind that yellow door—faux radio broadcasts and puppet shows, the painting of masterpieces and sewing of biking shorts, secret girl-club rituals and elaborate fort-building. My childhood, into which both sun and rain had fallen, had not been so different than most. Where I'd gotten into trouble was my insistence, for more than two decades, that every day had been rainbows and sunshine.

When I reached the patch of sidewalk across the street from my house, I stopped. Heaving and weeping, I wondered what a housewife on the block might think if she peeked out from behind her curtains and saw me. I didn't care. I had a *right* to some answers. Old 733 had an obligation to explain itself, to 'fess up. As I took in the full panorama, a soft, childlike voice inside of me insisted, "Bad things happened in there."

I don't know how long I remained glued to the sidewalk, taking in the scene of my childhood home like a sick voyeur. No new secrets were revealed, no forgotten memories recovered. None needed to be. The emotional information that I had been unable to manage in childhood had, apparently, been stored in my cells, held in my marrow.

Emotionally drained, I continued down the street, tracing the path Scott and I had taken to our first church.

Imaginable

I was still leaking tears as I limped passed the stone church, now smaller than I remembered. Glancing toward the bulwark, my gaze fell on the stately, framed signboard. By the looks of it, I figured it was the same one that had announced sermon titles several decades earlier. White plastic letters, five inches high, had been stuck into regular rows of black felt grooves.

Sunday's sermon title read, "A Scorpion for an Egg? Unimaginable!"

I stopped in my tracks. My hard drive clanked to a halt, making it difficult to process the words. Did it really say—did it really mean— what I thought it did? The degree from Princeton Seminary was of absolutely no help in that surreal moment.

It had been longer than I cared to remember since I had been mentally and spiritually pliable enough to receive a signboard message as God's personal word to me. Back in the day, I would have received all manner of signboards and misquoted Scripture verses as personal text messages from the Almighty. By the time I returned to the homeland, though, I was much more likely to disregard their wisdom as the fortune cookie or horoscope variety.

My exhausted mind clambered to complete the larger reference. Scorpions, scorpions . . . At last I placed it. "If your kid asks for bread, do you give him a rock? If she wants fish, do you hand her a live snake? *No way!*"

That was my memory of Jesus' answer.

Obviously, Jesus was wrong.

Rattled, I couldn't walk away from the church unsure that I'd truly understood the stinging reference.

I glanced at my watch: 4:28 p.m., Friday. Stumbling up the walkway, I tugged at the church's locked door. The deadbolt was one of the few reminders that it was no longer 1978. I was now keenly aware that I had crossed over some thin imaginary line that I'd thought had distinguished me as a competent spiritual guide. I was now among the ranks of other bleary, bloodshot church-knockers in search of assistance. Hesitantly, I rang the bell.

When a male voice answered through a speaker positioned above the doorbell, I weakly asked, "Are you the pastor who's preaching this Sunday?"

"No, I'm the associate pastor. Can I help you?"

"Um . . ." I said, trying to keep the tsunami of tears at bay, "I just had a question about the sermon title."

The kind voice offered, "Let me come down and let you in."

During the brief wait, I mused that the reason that church doors are locked must have something to do with me and my fellow hysterical cohorts.

The heavy wooden door opened. An African American man about my age appeared in the doorway. His jeans and baseball cap told me what I'd already suspected: the clergyman was ready for the weekend and had probably thought he'd made it home free. Sorry, pal, no such luck.

All the clothes and things that I needed for a raucous homecoming weekend were packed on my back. Some tears were drying on my cheeks. I looked exactly like the last person in the world I'd want to see if I were in his clerical sneakers. On better days, of course, I had been.

"Would you like to come in and sit down?" the pastor gently asked.

"No, I just have a quick question." My lips quivered as we stood in the church foyer. "I know this sounds crazy, but I was just wondering what the *sermon title* means."

He darted into a nearby office to grab a worship bulletin, glancing at it as he returned to where I stood. Fathers naturally want to give good gifts to their children, he assured me. He used more words than that, but that was the gist of it. Spotting a nearby Bible he flipped it open and nimbly located the passage. Reading it aloud, he assured me that God's gifts are even better than those.

He glanced up from the text. One look told him I wasn't buying it.

I desperately wanted to scream at the top of my lungs to the whole picturesque village, "For a father to give a scorpion to a child who needed an egg is *not* unimaginable. It is *incredibly* imaginable. Fathers *do* give bad gifts to their children!"

The unspoken gospel corollary—that God is naturally like human fathers—was painfully obvious both to me and to my makeshift shepherd. Instinctively, he added, "If you've received bad gifts, you need to know that God's love is not like that."

Though my orthodoxy agreed, my insides railed, "Well, of course God's love is like that!" Numbness failing, the defenses I'd developed to protect God's goodness were melting away with the season's snow. I was alone in a scorpion desert.

The reverend offered me a Bible and tried to show me where to find the passage. I assured him I could find it. The graduate degree, I mused to myself, was good for at least that much. I thanked him politely and wandered back out toward the street.

What was so ludicrous is that I could have preached the wallpaper off a wall about God's great love for his children. I had and I did. I even meant it. Though my head and my heart were certain of God's extravagant love, my deep insides had no idea.

Maternal Signboard

A few months later, after I'd returned to Durham, I spotted a church signboard near my adult home that was clearly past its one-week expiration date. The fact that the words lingered on a full eight days after Mother's Day made the ill-fated message seem all the more cruel: "God couldn't be everywhere, so he made mothers."

It was hard to know which half of the aphorism was more offensive: that God was sorely limited in his ability to be present to children, or that in the divine absence, God appointed the *particular* mother of whatever reader was driving by to do his bidding. Who comes up with these things is what I wanted to know. And where are the theology police when we need them?

Could an inadequate God really have appointed the mother of every driver to execute his wily schemes? I couldn't help but think of the long line of maternal absences, chosen and unchosen, in both my biological and adoptive families. The words seemed to mock, "Since God couldn't forsake you personally, seeing as he was busy with other matters, he made mothers to do it instead." It's a wonder that there are any remaining believers at all in Durham, North Carolina, who have traveled that disconcerting route on their way to work or school or to their own churches with other clever signboards.

To be fair, some drivers-by I'm sure had mothers who represented to them aspects of a faithful and gracious God. My own birth mother had shown me what a Creator God was like, and my adoptive mother had shown me God as generous Provider.

Another reader, though, was probably beaten by an angry mother who was beaten by her own angry mother. Another was exposed to sexual abuse under an averted maternal gaze. One lived in poverty with a mother who was, more often than not, drunk. Another, dwelling in affluence, experienced a mother whose pill-popping started early and finished late.

Did a misguided signboard volunteer truly believe that these mothers were divinely appointed to inflict fear, anger, sadness and loneliness in God's stead? Or could it be that mothers and children all stand in need of redemption by a completely different Parent altogether?

Meanie God

The coupling of the two signboards had jangled open the old infection that still festered inside. As my own early losses continued to bubble up from the recesses of my heart, I experienced a debilitating depression. Some days I was bedridden with sadness. I had no energy to create. I had little motivation to exercise.

One day Peter encouraged me to go walking, thinking how it had often improved my mood. I patiently explained to him that when I was *depressed*—a very sterile and clinical word, I think, to describe what it is to wallow in one's own personal pit of hell—I could not even move my legs or arms, let alone approach anything resembling my target heart rate. I also warned him that if any friendly, gardening neighbor dared to speak to me I would either burst into tears or stab her with the rusty tip of her own dirty shovel. No one wants that.

Daringly, Peter still shuffled me out the door where I curled up in our carport, out of sight, so no neighbor could see me. There I plotted routes to exit my neighborhood without anyone I knew smiling or waving or speaking. Once I had targeted a safe escape, hidden behind the cover of a passing street sweeper, I scurried out from behind our car to go for a walk.

Then I let God have it. *Why am I in so much pain? Why won't this end? What sort of a meanie Father God are you, anyway?* And there it was. The string of questions that began with *me, me, me* always ended up with *you, you, you!* The deep conflict in my bones, that I had assumed I'd known the answer to but had never dared to ask, was: *Are you like this string of human fathers I've experienced, or are you something else? Because, quite frankly, I'm not seeing how you're very different.*

Are you like the first father who couldn't be bothered to lay eyes on me? Are you like the daddy I loved who left me? Are you like the ill-equipped stepfather who left me? Maybe you're like that first father who, decades later, didn't even want the second chance he'd been given. This accusing line of attack could really go on for quite a while. *I hurt. Where were you?*

As I walked during those days, I begged God to show me the one face in childhood that might have been altogether *for* me when things were crazy. While there had been many faces that rejoiced with me, I searched for the one that grieved with me. I looked for the adult countenance that reflected, "I'm so sorry, baby, that you experienced that. I'm so sorry he left. I'm so sorry I left. I wonder if you felt scared? I wonder if you felt sad? You deserve more, sweetheart. You are worth it."

In the absence of those eyes and that voice, I just assumed that I had deserved everything I got. Children learn what they live. Every caregiver along the broken way had insisted they loved me. I raised my fist and demanded, "What is love anyway, you crazy Love-God!?!?"

Bad Stuff in the Book

I even started to read and listen to words in the Bible a little differently. I began to wonder what they would have sounded like when I was younger if I had been completely honest, if I hadn't felt the desperate need to protect God. In the calligraphy-adorned Bible that I had received when I was eight, John 3:16 had been neatly squared in penciled lines. One day I let my inner child loose with it.

For God so loved the world . . .

So far, so good.

that he gave his only Son . . .

Wait, wait. Hold up. God gave up his Son just like regular parents? Like when they give the kid up for adoption? Or because they drink too much and can't take care of the kid anymore? Or commit crimes and end up in prison? Or because they like their dumb boyfriend more than they like their own kid? It just seems like God shouldn't do that stuff. Really, how can anyone trust this guy? *Loving the world* must mean he recycles and eats vegan because, frankly, he's not doing a bang-up job of loving his Son. I guess I should just be thankful I'm not *his* kid.

so that everyone who believes in him should not perish but have eternal life

Yada, yada, yada. AM I THE ONLY ONE IN THIS RELIGION WHO CAN *READ?!*

With the cracking of my heart's shell, something had shifted, causing me to reconsider what was never meant to be up for deliberation.

I was still mulling it over one morning while perusing some stimulating cereal-box trivia that reported all the words for *snow* that the Alaskan Inuit language contains. Although I was entirely satisfied with the singular English *snow* for the white stuff that falls from the sky, I decided that I was becoming increasing disturbed by the paucity of English words for *love*. One was not nearly enough for those of us who have weathered complicated emotional climates.

In seminary we'd studied the three Greek words for "love," words I had seen for years in the margin notes of my study Bible. *Philia*, brotherly love, was nice, but brothers leave for college across the country. *Eros*, romantic love, clearly clouded people's good judgment in relationships. I was willing to admit that *agape*, a self-giving love, had some potential. Although I knew what it looked like in the flannel-board ghetto where Jesus lived, I'm not sure I could have identified it in my own neighborhood. Sorting through the primal shards of my early experience, what passed as love began to look less and less like what it was supposed to. As the blinders were removed, I realized that for years I had extrapolated what love meant from my human experience of it. We all do.

Some ghost birth father had agreed to relinquish me for adoption. I was assured by my adoptive parents that he had made this choice because he "loved" me. The father on whom I depended and who I adored left me to take a job across the country when I was six years old. He, too, assured me he "loved" me. The threatening chorus of his replacement, my stepfather, haunted me: "Nobody loves you like I love you." Somehow I only caught the first three words.

I'm no trained linguist, but there have got to be better words to use in these situations than *love*. This is what had been so crazy-making—that what I'd been told did not match the reality that my heart, soul, mind and body had experienced and known to be true. Someone who loved me abandoned me. Someone who loved me left me behind. Someone who loved me threatened my safety.

I was disgusted that I continued to experience love's ill effects in my marriage and in my friendships. I was fearful, guarded, mistrusting, sad, furious—all because of that dodgy thing that others had called *love*.

This was why I had the vested interest in vocab. I decided that there really needs to be an English expression that means, "You are precious, but I'm unable to meet your needs right now." There needs to be a way to say, "You are worthy, but I am struggling for my own survival here." We need a word for, "I am not able to be *for* you in the way that you really need me to be at this time."

As I was still trying to put my finger on that slippery word, another forced its way into my cells' lexicon.

Unmotherless Son

Although I had never been one to fall prey to the second deadly sin in its more socially sanctioned expressions, such as coveting my friends' designer handbags or footwear, I did envy old friends from high school who were adopting a son from Haiti. I'd recently reconnected with them on Facebook. My heart thrilled for this one who was about to become kin.

With dinner in the oven, I dropped into my office chair to check e-mail. After deleting a few, I clicked open my friend's most recent adoption update.

We have been told that when we visit him in Haiti we will be able to meet his birth family and see where he grew up.

Until that moment I hadn't been aware of international adoptions in which any members of the extended family were involved. What a good gift for that boy, I mused. I fantasized that he would stay in touch over the years with a grandparent or distant aunt.

I continued scrolling down the message.

Then when it is time for him to leave Haiti and join our family, we actually will have someone else escort him from Haiti to our home in Denver.

I was perplexed, wondering why the couple wouldn't make the trip once more to bring their son home. Staring blindly at the computer screen, I wondered why my friends would choose not to travel with their new son during such a precarious passage? My mind searched to fill the void. As if to address the cartoon-bubble question mark over my head, the e-mail continued.

I hear that trip can be pretty tough with the moms saying goodbye to their children in front of you.

The birth mothers? Saying goodbye? To their *children? In front of adoptive parents?* The world around me and the one within stopped spinning. Every neural pathway in my body jammed up as I attempted to process the information I'd read.

Lifeless, I went through the motions of calling the family to the table, serving food and eating. After dinner I returned to my study and to my friend's e-mail. While Peter finished rinsing dinner dishes in the kitchen, I bellowed the words to him, in hopes that doing so might make what seemed absurd more sensible.

"How could a kid with *parents* be adopted?" I demanded of him and of the world. "Nothing about that seems right. Orphans are adopted. Parents raise their children. End of story."

My husband listened patiently to my tirade, resisting the urge to offer sane comment. Dishes continued to clink in the kitchen sink as I began making a mental list of authorities I deemed to be in a position to confirm or deny this atrocity. One was a well-known adoption advocate with connections to a number of leading figures in the national adoption community. Another was a local nurse who had been a missionary to Haiti and who worshiped at our church. This woman had devoted herself to ministry with Haitian Christians and traveled there frequently. The third was an indigenous Haitian pastor who was widely respected in Haiti and abroad. Surely these people could shed light on what seemed, to my mind, an incredibly unjust situation.

I felt certain that the fervent adoption advocate would storm, "You're kidding! That's outrageous! We're going to let the world know that this is happening!" I could clearly picture her opening her laptop while assuring me, "I'm posting it on the listserve right now. We're going to get some action on this." Perhaps we could coauthor a fiery article and get some national attention.

And surely, if the nurse-missionary knew of this situation, she would choke out, "That's horrible! I have never heard of such a thing." She would be visibly touched by the suffering of the people she loved. With her compassionate heart for the Haitians, I imagined her reasoning, "If it happens, it must be rare." Her face, in my mind's eye, bore the agony these families had endured.

The final champion to make an appearance in my vision was the wise pastor. With solemn countenance, I could almost hear him confirming in a thick Haitian accent, "Yes, it is true. Our people are so very poor. Parents see this as a way for their children to survive. It is very sad indeed." Then he would describe his church's work among the poor: "We provide support for these families, but so many are devastated by poverty. They see the orphanages as their only option."

Needed Rest

The kitchen was now silent and dark. Though I heard Peter in our bedroom, settling in for the night, I continued perusing the lengthy e-mail. I scrolled through the requisite account, which attempted to explain the incomprehensible.

> I guess in Haiti the moms are so desperate for someone to care for and feed their kids that they are thankful to get the children into an orphanage and it becomes quite the competing business for who has the best orphanage, et cetera. The moms are then still able to visit the children . . .

Enough. I tottered off toward bed now, sensing a new distance from my friend. The magical thread knitting us together had too quickly unraveled. Was I crazy? Would others react to the formation of their family as strongly as I?

I knew they wouldn't. Blind to a child's unfathomable loss, the well-meaning would say, "Bless you. It's such a good thing you've done. Your reward is in heaven." My friend would politely deny it, yet some of the warmth would linger.

Still unsettled, I climbed under the covers. I had no reason to question the integrity of these friends. Fluffing my pillow, I tried to convince myself that it was all for the best. Thoughts of terrified children being ripped from maternal arms and shipped to what, in their experience, was akin to another planet nagged at me. I wanted to believe that under such grave circumstances all this could, somehow, be warranted. I tried to rationalize the seismic emotional and cultural rupture endured by these older children as legitimate. At last I nodded off with my mind still scanning for resolution, now furiously spinning to resolve the conundrum that so suddenly and forcefully demanded my attention and energy.

The bedside clock glowed 2:37 a.m.

With the clarity that only middle-of-the-night awakenings afford, I realized that my indignation had been projected onto unwitting pale-skinned and dark-skinned players. In that strangely lucid moment, it became clear that my angst was not only about them.

I, too, had been relinquished while my own parents were still living. The few brief paragraphs delivered on adoption-agency letterhead had simply failed to make them *seem* real. Essentially, they had been dead to me.

My choice of "expert witnesses"—advocate, nurse and pastor—voiced the rage, confusion and sadness that were in fact my own. The adult child curled beneath my covers had lived too long under the blanket of an unconscious fear. For too long I had quelled the expression of my authentic anger, doubt and grief. In my deepest places I was—understandably, I think—unsure that those around me could tolerate my truest self.

Those three witnesses bore such striking resemblance to another Trinity of authoritative friends at my disposal. The first is the fiery one who advocates on my behalf. The next is the human one who hurts for the hurt of his people. Finally, I saw the face of the paternal one who longs for justice to reign on earth as it does in heaven.

The three I had invoked to judge my friend became, after all, the One I needed.

We would, before long, become better acquainted.

- nine -

CLAIMED BY
THE GOOD TRIBE

During my hardest days, I orchestrated my Sunday morning church maneuvers like I was on Air Force One, secretly dipping into and out of wartime Iraq. Because friendly Sunday school chatter was more than I could bear, I would time my departure from home, one mile from church, just as class began. Avoiding parking lot pleasantries was just a fringe benefit. Once in the building, having quickly dropped Zoë off at Sunday school, I would slide into the classroom, head down, as if I were already listening intently to the lesson. For forty minutes I would sit in a daze, nodding occasionally in rote agreement, overwhelmed by emotional pain.

In order to avoid the cheerful crush of the rush hour between Sunday school and the beginning of worship, I would reverently depart four minutes before the end of class. I would march out of the room importantly, as if I were on my way to save a life in the church nursery. Slipping out of the building, I would walk toward the parking lot, then past it and continue away from church. Having meticulously calculated the time between my departure and five minutes after the beginning of worship, I would split the difference walking nine minutes north on Broad Street and then nine minutes back south again.

The crowded rear entrance of the sanctuary, guarded by two cheerful deacons, always felt much too dangerous to attempt an entry. Instead, I would march purposely into the front of the sanctuary, find my first-row spot and pivot around to face the pulpit. There my face, already bleeding unauthorized tears, would be mostly hidden from others. There I would endure the entire service, and then, during the closing prayer, the whole sequence of bobbing and weaving would begin again as I made my carefully planned escape.

Every Sunday was like this, avoiding friendly fire. On my best worst days, I would dodge everyone. On the worst ones, I might catch a grenade from a well-meaning library volunteer thumbing through a stack of overdue book notices or a friend who was happy to see me.

The last place I wanted to be when I was in so much pain was in church. Even at the time, I knew that my desperate resistance to human contact with Christ's body was absolutely devilish.

Law Stuff

Like those of my parents' generation who can pinpoint their whereabouts when they heard that John F. Kennedy had been shot, I can still see the stretch of road I was traveling in Durham, North Carolina, when I heard the news that would rock *my* world.

"Mitch and Jessica won't know for certain that the baby will be theirs for a while," Peter explained, "It's some legal thing."

While driving, Peter had been telling me about friends who were in the process of adopting a baby of Native American heritage. I hung on his words with rapt attention.

"Legal thing?" I queried. "What does that mean?"

We drove past the campus of Duke University as Peter casually spit out the bit of legal trivia. "I guess when a child with Cherokee blood is given up for adoption," he reported flatly, "the tribe's rights to raise the child aren't terminated for six months."

Immediately, my heart rate quickened.

"How much Cherokee?" I demanded. "Is it 50 percent? Or 25 percent?" I badgered anxiously. "What about other Native American tribes? Do they have the same deal?"

As my husband and I continued to drive down Main Street, I ruminated over the fact that Pam had told me during our first phone conversation that her great-great-great-grandfather had been Native American. I quickly did the math in my head.

As Peter continued to babble about our adopting friends, I silently began to wonder whether my .8 percent Native American blood would qualify me to participate in the same program. Could *I* be claimed and raised by the tribe? As an adult, I realized it was unlikely. Yet an odd seed of hope had been sown in my heart. The obscure factoid from U.S. family law allowed me, at last, to imagine new possibilities.

A vision of the good tribe coming to the hospital to claim me as an infant flooded my mind. A colorful, proud clan of brave protectors and wise nurturers would have swooped in to call me their own. I fantasized about growing up among a people who were, in good times and bad, *for* me. No matter what outside interference threatened the tribe, we would have weathered nature's storms together. In an instant, this wonderful window of possibility had flown open.

"Peter!" I blurted, "The tribe could have come for me!"

The blank look on his face told me he had not yet caught the vision.

Lots of Smiles

Although my thirty-fourth birthday fell on the same day of the week on which I'd been born, Friday the thirteenth, I had no reason to expect that the creepy omen of doom would cast a shadow on my special day. Every birthday I'd ever celebrated, on Tuesdays and Fridays and Sundays, had gone off without a hitch. Even in the midst of that difficult season I planned to pony up with a glimmering smile, dramatic present-opening and voracious cake-scarfing. The strategy had worked for more than three decades, and I saw no reason to switch it up. In fact, a box of fading photos will testify that for thirty-three birthdays I had smiled.

Number one was, of course, the requisite, incredibly cute, cake-smeared smile from the wooden high chair.

Seven showed a buck-toothed girl picnicking at the hallowed "swim party."

The plastic grin of number fourteen belied my deep humiliation that I and all my friends had just returned from the amusement park and borne witness to an embarrassing domestic situation.

Number twenty, with Geni, was snapped by Jane or Terry at a pizza parlor in South Africa. They would also be the ones to offer me my first legal drink in the States the following summer on our free-wheeling road trip. Another smile.

Wide-eyed twenty-seven was clicked the moment I came home from work to find that Peter and a few friends had surprised me with the trampoline I'd dreamed of since number seven.

All those smiles had been documented for posterity. I could point to them as the proof that for thirty-three birthdays, I had smiled. I could spread them out for anyone who might have seen me on the eve of thirty-four to prove that what happened that night was an aberration.

I had never been one of these women who starts dropping hints six months early that her birthday is on the way. Neither had I been one to avoid or deny an upcoming birthday. It's not like I was a supermodel whose livelihood depended on a wrinkle-free complexion, tight abs or gravity-defying breasts. I had achieved the dreams of my grandmother's generation: the husband, the child, the home in the suburbs. I had fulfilled my own ambitions, completing graduate school, working in several rewarding positions and starting countless failed business ventures that were really fun. I think my overall satisfaction with my life is why the eve of my thirty-fourth birthday took me completely off-guard.

In a pensive moment on the couch, I returned in my imagination to the moments around my debut. I'd learned from Pam that, per the practice of the day, she had been sedated during labor and had been unconscious when I was born. The foster family who would care for me during those first few weeks hadn't known I was even on the way. My adoptive parents wouldn't set eyes on me for over two more weeks. There were no grandparents waiting on pins and needles in the lobby. No uncles handed out pink-wrapper cigars. No cousins waited anxiously with signs and balloons.

That mental thumbnail sketch quickly gave way to heaving sobs of despair as I sat beside Peter on the couch. At last I spit out the gut-wrenching realization, "No one wanted me to be born."

That's not to say that anyone tried to thwart my arrival. No one did. But at my birth no one had been delighted. No one had rejoiced. No one had been insanely giddy that I had finally made my way into the world. No one had strapped me securely to their back, tightly bound in a leather papoose, to proudly parade me around the village. I was tribeless.

I couldn't help but remember the cacophony of rejoicing at Zoë's birth. In anticipation of her arrival we'd been showered with gifts, cards and phone calls. The morning after I delivered her, L'Anni and my childhood friend Hillary rushed to the hospital. Church members brought tiny monogrammed baby shoes and hand-painted artwork to match the nursery. Even in the awful baby warmer that separates children from their naturally warm mothers, Peter had assured Zoë of his reliable presence. Loved ones who came to welcome our daughter had communicated, with face and body and voice, what so many individuals, at many ages, long to hear, "Hooray! You're here!"

As I returned in my mind to my own entry into the world, I could not see the human faces that had delighted in my arrival. Instead, on the difficult evening before my birthday, I was overwhelmed by absence.

I was still weeping beside Peter on the couch when the phone rang. After four rings the machine picked up. It was Seth. I turned to Peter and moaned, "I just *can't.*" I couldn't answer the phone. Seth's perky babbling was oil to my watery despair. Peter understood and stayed beside me.

"Hi, Margot and Peter! This is Seth. I know it's the twelfth but I just wanted to call and be the first to say, 'Happy Birthday!'"

As anyone knows, that should have been the end of it. Leave a quick message and hang up. That, however, was not the end of it. Instead, Seth blathered on and on and on and on. About not so much.

"Peter, am I a jerk?" I asked my husband. "I really know I should pick up, but I just can't. I'm a mess." Another sympathetic nod.

Seth went on for so long—I hadn't known the answering machine had that much recording space—that I eventually got up off my sick couch and weakly lifted the receiver.

"Hi, it's me," I choked out. Seth had been through so much with me that I realized that it was fitting that I tell him about my horrible birthday eve realization. I'm pretty sure I heard him wince in pain with me.

"I'm *so* glad you were born," he confirmed affectionately. A little voice whispered in my ear that he *had* to say that. Then a true—and actually believable—voice insisted that he meant it.

Who even calls the night before?

The next morning, still stinging, I pulled myself together as best I could. I dressed like the person I wanted to be. That year's photo shows me wearing orange and salmon capri pants with a bright pink T-shirt. Smiling.

When Scott called to wish me a happy birthday, I shared my hard revelation with him. He listened intently.

"You know, Margs," he finally ventured, "I think that God uses labor and delivery nurses in times like this." I pictured a Native American midwife, in blue scrubs and long black braids, cradling me on behalf of the whole tribe. Scott had articulated the very thing I had begun to suspect about God's unlikely plan. God's own care could be made known through human eyes, ears and arms, just as it had been actualized through Moses. And *to* baby Moses, for that matter.

When my birthday evening rolled around, the phone rang again. Peter grabbed it. A true extrovert, he is strangely vivified by crowds and parties and ringing telephones. He handed it to me.

"Hey Margot, it's Tony. Lynda and I just wanted to call to say that we're glad you were born."

Now this was just getting ridiculous. My friends Tony and Lynda had gone out of town for the weekend and had *still* remembered me.

Through the unwitting lips of Seth, Scott and Tony, the voice of Another was speaking truth to the lies that my experience had spoken to my heart.

Pink Post-It Note

I knew that the birthday card that had been carefully written in my grandmother's hand had been bought, prompted and mailed by my grandfather. I had heard, through family members, that she was developing the symptoms of Alzheimer's. When I arrived in Indiana to celebrate her summer birthday, my grandmother was delighted to see me. As gracious as ever, I immediately noticed that she was still very adept at managing social situations. Scott and I watched as she played with our children in my aunt's living room.

Nodding toward our grandmother, Scott mused, "She really is a ma-triarch." His tone hinted at some essential quality beyond simple lon-gevity. I could hear in his voice that not everyone who lives a really long time qualifies for the impressive distinction. I mentally searched for any other reigning matriarchs. It was not a long list. Actually, just Rose Ken-nedy and the Queen of England.

"So, what makes her a matriarch?" I asked. Now I was curious.

He quickly answered, "She'd take a bullet for any one of us."

He was right. She would.

My grandmother wandered into the living room to find Scott and me chatting. Her brow furrowed with concern. "Margot, honey, how are your feet doing?" she asked. For the years that my feet had been injured she had always been keenly interested in their well-being. She had duti-fully sent every article and advertisement for the relief of foot pain that fell under her gaze. Although I had assured her many times that since I instituted the morning routine they had been relatively fine, she contin-ued to ask. To care.

I was impressed. She couldn't remember what she'd had for breakfast, but somehow she reached deep into the recesses of her heart's memory to ask about my feet.

Scott wandered away to leave us to our girl talk.

"Wow, thanks for asking. That is so sweet. They're still the same. If I stretch them before I bear weight in the morning, I can walk fine all day. I don't run, but I manage walking just fine. I'm careful to wear support-ive shoes."

"Oh sweetie, I think about your feet all the time. I just want you to take such good care of them. Feet are so important."

"Thanks, Grandmother. I'm taking good care of them."

"And how's your sister . . . ?" She searched for my sister's name. This lapse I have never begrudged her. Kristen, Rick's daughter from his second marriage, was ten years my junior.

"Kristen," I volunteered. "She's good. She is taking the year off before she begins medical school. I saw her last year at Grandpa Fred's funeral and she really is a sweetheart. She's a neat young lady. Thanks for asking."

She seemed satisfied. She had always been terribly impressed by doctors.

It appeared to me that my grandmother was in much better shape than everyone had indicated. She had asked about my feet *and* my stepsister. I saw no signs of decline.

While we were chatting, my aunt invited us to dinner. We all stood around the table, joined hands and bowed our heads while my grandfather prayed. Following the prayer we filled our plates with lasagna, salad and bread in the kitchen and returned to find seats at the table.

Rushing to elbow out my cousin Joanna for the prized seat, I plunked down next to my grandmother. With fork poised, she turned to me to pick up the conversation where we'd left off in the living room. "Now tell me all about everything in your life," she began warmly. I knew it wasn't small talk. She genuinely wanted to know.

I filled her in on the details and then pivoted a little to listen to one of Joanna's crazy stories about her young son.

No longer in the spotlight, my grandmother reached into her shirt pocket and pulled out a small slip of paper. It was a square, pink Post-It note. After reading it, she tipped it over gently to rest face-down on the table, still held by her thinning fingers. I turned back to glimpse her discreetly slipping the note up the sleeve of her blouse.

"Now . . ." she queried hesitantly, "Have I asked you about your feet?" She glanced nervously toward the paper.

In that moment I realized that she had had a script. Not only had there been cue cards all along, she now had no idea that she had asked me the same thing thirteen minutes earlier.

The reports were true.

"You know what, you *did*. Thank you," I said. My tone suggested that it could have been three or four years ago that she asked, and that whatever my answer had been at the time was equally difficult for me to recall.

"They're about the same," I reported afresh. "I have to stretch them before I can stand up in the morning, and that gets them in shape for the day. It's really not that bad."

She peeked again at the note. "And . . ." she began.

"Let me see that thing!" I blurted, taking the paper from her hand. Carefully penciled in her beautiful script, the note read: "Margot: How are your feet? How is your half-sister? Where is she and what is she do-ing now?"

I was completely blown away. How could she have had the foresight to write these down *and* the good fortune to find them? "Hey, gimmee that thing. I want to keep it," I teased with a grin.

She laughed nervously, trying to protest. The matriarch of our tribe was exposed.

Lowering my voice, I begged, "Please, please, please. It makes me feel so loved. Please?"

Smiling, she conceded.

I tucked the note into my wallet to preserve as a lasting reminder: her unflagging love for me was stronger than the power of death.

In the Silence

When an invitation to a silent weekend retreat at a local convent arrived in the mailbox one day, I jumped at the opportunity. Although I was about as friendly with silence as I was with emotion, I dared to hope that I might encounter God there in a transforming way.

The weekend came, and I blew it. I did. I was unable to manage silence. In an undisguised attempt to point fingers, I blame the retreat planners. Specifically, they left a big basket of art supplies in the convent's common room, inviting anyone to partake. That kind gesture was like offering brownies laced with marijuana to a woman in rehab. Some women, unaddicted ones, would have—and did—find it helpful. In no time, though, I fell right off that silence wagon and got very busy. I didn't *talk*, but I also did not embrace the silence. Instead, as I listened for God's voice in the quiet, in Scripture and even in my dreams, I proceeded to paint what I heard and saw.

In a rare moment of actual silence, I was quietly walking a labyrinth in a grassy open area of the convent property. Suddenly, a vision filled my mind. At first glance, the mental picture looked like a huge ball of yarn. Apparently God loved me enough to stoop to using craft supplies to get my attention. Covered in endless bands, though, the ball was not wound in yarn, but in wide strips of colorful satin ribbon. The wrapped sphere was a brilliant ball of rainbow colors, smooth bands winding round on top of one another. I knew immediately what it represented.

It was my heart.

Although I couldn't see beneath the satin bandages, I knew that my soft, pink, healing heart was under there. At last the hard shell with which I had protected myself for so long was gone. Since that first fissure that Isaiah had birthed, pieces of shell had continued to be chiseled, cracked and licked away. The process had been painful. In the vision, though, I'd seen the strips with which God had bound my hurting heart, gently swaddling it to health. Like a newborn. True to form, I immediately scurried back to the quiet of my cell to paint that gorgeous ribbon ball.

To this day that painting reminds me that, unaware, I'd been under the care of one reliable Medicine Man all along.

The Clan

Despite such moments of encouragement, I continued to perseverate on the divine possibility that the tribe might have come for me as an infant. When I returned home from my quiet-ish weekend, I continued walking and searching. As I did, I started to catch glimpses of the faces in the tribe that had been used in my life to make real for me God's steadfast presence.

I pictured my brother, Scott, whose brave heart held for me the love of a mother and the hope of a father, the exuberance of a sister and the joy of angels.

I saw the expressions on my grandparents' faces as they exclaimed, "Honey, we were *just* thinking about you!"

There was the gracious countenance of Seth, who knew my whole story and who cared deeply for me. His parents too.

I saw the many, mighty prayer warriors who'd gone to battle on my behalf.

I saw my mother's frame bent over mine, gently stroking my hair, as I lay in bed with chicken pox.

I saw my dad's face, sober, as he labored over an elaborate chart diagramming a sequence for my ten colors of nail polish.

I saw my mother's husband, Don, tireless in his delight in me.

I saw Geni's and Isaiah's faces and heard them simultaneously chime, "I love you, girl," and "Lub you, Auntie Gogo." When we had first met, Geni's unconditional love had taken me by surprise. For years I had so guarded my heart that I had not been able to receive her good gift. I slowly realized that in her enduring friendship, love had slowly been soaking into my bones.

I saw Pam's beaming middle-aged countenance, convinced, beyond all reason I think, that I was simply the cat's meow.

I recognized Tony and Lynda, who had cared for me more times than I even liked to remember.

I saw the skilled therapist whose face reflected the truth of my worth. Another warrior.

And of course Peter's fantastic face appeared in the montage.

##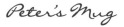

I love Peter's face. It's pretty much *all* facial features. There's just enough other stuff, skin and bone, to hold together those fabulous eyes, ears, nose and mouth. It is a particularly fitting face for someone who notices, listens and senses so well before speaking. (This is when he's not operating a motor vehicle. When he's behind the wheel of a car, all those nice things I just said fly right out the rolled-down window.)

I am grateful that it is the face to which Zoë has been privileged to turn. One evening when she was a toddler, she was playing under the dining room table while Peter and I ate our dinner. Standing suddenly, she cracked her head on the corner of the wooden table. Before the wail escaped her lips, her daddy's face contorted into an agonized grimace.

"Ouch!" he reflected. "That hurts!"

Someone entering the room would have looked at his face and naturally assumed that *he* had been the one who'd gotten knocked upside the head. Cradling our girl and gazing into her wet eyes, his compassionate features assured her, "Daddy knows how much it hurts." I watched in amazement. Though she still cried, she didn't do it quite so loud, or for quite as long, as she would have without her father's presence. Soon she was back on the floor, playing. The whole healing scene was a thing of beauty to me.

Many others have experienced this gift through Peter's pastoral ministry. One Sunday I carefully watched Peter leading worship. I always noticed him up there, blathering on, but this time I really paid attention. Predictably, the prayer of confession, sermon and his unplanned wisecracks were all up to par. I took particular notice that morning, though, of his mug as he received the congregation's prayer requests. He has always resisted the pastoral role of "professional Christian," and he has worked instead to empower others to be God's agents in the world. Voiced prayers from members of the congregation during worship was part of that genius plan.

One woman stood to ask for prayers for her sons, who were chronically ill. As he received her request, Peter's face fell with the heartbreak that this mother and others must surely endure. When a young father announced the birth of his first son, Peter's face erupted into delight. When another woman asked the congregation to pray for her grieving aunt at the end of a fifty-three-year-long marriage, Peter's expression reflected an anguished ache.

God has used that face to care for many, not only in front of gathered worshipers but beside hospital beds and funeral plots, behind chip-littered tailgates and Little League backstops.

So how lucky are Zoë and I to have him in our very own tribe?

I Am

The face I continued to find the most difficult to visualize in the good tribe was a paternal one. While a few men appeared in the composite image of the tribe, which was evolving in my heart and mind, I was still looking for the one who had been altogether *for* me. After several weeks of gathering thumbnails for my virtual album, I still had one important page to fill.

"I can see all these faithful faces," I explained to Peter in our kitchen, "but I'm just not seeing the Father face that I'm after. I catch glimpses, but not the whole enchilada. I just can't see it."

This was the huge, Paleolithic bone I had to pick with God. Week after week I walked and picked, continuing to scan for the person who, in good times and bad, had been *for* me. By my estimation I logged approximately 461 miles searching for the answer.

As I walked, I scrolled endlessly through my Rolodex of the usual suspects: birth parents, foster parents, adoptive parents, stepparents. Invariably some absence or transgression, some expression of being human, would prompt me to move on in my search for the perfect face. Birth parents, foster parents, adoptive parents, stepparents. Where was that face that had not failed?

The agonizing search came to an end one day near the intersection of Knox and Ruffin. I had stomped away from home to get some exercise as I'd done so many other days, clenching my fists and demanding answers. Then, like the foot-stretching miracle before it, the answer suddenly dropped into my consciousness (with the wonderful serendipity of two gumballs showing up for one coin!):

"I am."

Instinctively, I knew the words to be true in my bones. I knew they were meant for me.

"I am." If it had been a Lifetime movie, and not my own actual life, it would have been the moment the orchestra would have begun playing to signal a satisfying denouement to my quest.

"I am."

I realize that skeptics could debate where those words came from. I'm entirely willing to waive credit if one day I realize that I stole them from a greeting card or bumper sticker. If I'd seen them on a vanity license plate they would have read: I M 4 U.

When Moses asked "Who?" he got the same old answer I did. Maybe I just read it in Scripture. Yet in that moment those ancient, typeset words lifted off the Bible's inanimate pages to satisfy the deepest thirst of my heart. The efficacy of the atonement was entirely dependent on the person behind the words. The I AM who met the world's deep yearning as bread, light, truth and life came to me, in that moment, as I AM.

"I am *for you*, Margot." I am *for* you.

The four words felt too good to be true. Were they truly from God? It was more likely, I reasoned, that the dam holding back my ocean of neediness had sprung a leak, and that the beach ball wish of what I most *longed* to hear had popped uncontrollably into my consciousness. I was keenly aware of that possibility. I'm no sucker.

Closing my eyes, I looked toward the Speaker for confirmation. Seeing the face of Christ, the sense I had about him was "emptiness." Holy emptiness. That seemed like an odd impression, I thought. Not something you would want to advertise on a church signboard, that's for sure.

And although I'm much more comfortable with the empty crosses hanging in Protestant churches than the ones in Roman Catholic churches that have Jesus pinned there like a helpless insect, in that moment I saw Jesus on the cross.

Of course.

My angry, clenched fist now released, I found in my palm the key to home. It was cross-shaped, the place where all absence had been redeemed. Of course. This was the One who chose to empty himself in order to be completely *for* me. A fatherly voice assured me: "It's what I do. It's who I am. I do not seek my own life at your expense. I'm completely for you."

I am *for* you.

Hard to believe, that.

The tribe's Chief, who I had previously suspected might just be the most horrible cosmic child abuser ever, assured me, "I am one, Father, Son and Holy Spirit. *I* came down and gave *my own life* for you."

I wasn't sure if I could take it all in.

My Presbyterian brain kept chewing and chewing on that I AM revelation. Had I really heard that? Perhaps it was not only real in the flannelgraph ghetto. Could it possibly be true, bone-true, for me?

During the days in which I continued to chew on that gumball idea, our church offered its regular monthly healing service. Dutifully I presented myself, out of habit more than faithfulness. Apparently, that was enough. As I stepped forward to join the circle of family gathered around the communion table, I was still wondering about that I AM.

As the holy bread touched my lips, moist with spilled blood, I felt at last that I'd been claimed. I belonged to the Chief. I had his blood. Though the reality of his goodness would need to be more fully digested over time, I knew, in my bones, that it was true. Most teachers say that there's no stupid question. As I tasted his broken body and swallowed his spilled blood, though, I still felt a little embarrassed to have asked whether or not he was *for* me. What a suddenly silly question.

There, in the church sanctuary, one of the congregation's graying elders laid his kind hands on my head and prayed. He was married and had three children of his own. At the time I did not know him well. He stood beside his wife, who, with another friend, had prayed me through some of my darkest days. A physician by profession, his medically trained hands became for me, in that moment, the Lord's own healing hands.

In this man's compassionate voice, I heard Christ's own prayers for me. As he anointed my forehead, speaking God's blessing to me, God confirmed, "Margot, my girl, I *have* come. I have come in my people for you."

It was true. The tribe *had* come. And the tribe was *for* me.

Super Bubble

Hanging prominently in our hallway art gallery is the most fabulous, yummy and amazing piece of liturgical art one can possibly imagine. Lynda and her son Conner made it for me.

At first glance, you just see a chalice and loaf of bread resting on a table. When you get up close you can see that it has been made entirely out of Super Bubble gum wrappers. Fields of blue, red and yellow have been artfully patched into the forms of bread and cup using the flattened wrappers.

I am always tickled when visitors peruse the visual offerings in our hallway. When they pause in front of Lynda and Conner's framed masterpiece, I watch their faces, waiting for that moment when they finally realize the fields of color have been created entirely from trash.

"Look, look!" I badger. "Look at what it's called!"

In the bottom, right-hand corner, beside the artists' initials, is the title of the work: "More Than We Can Chew."

- ten -

GOD'S COOL TATTOO

Wouldn't that last little bit be a nice place for the story to end? Nine tidy chapters. A perfect square. A few tears and a moving emotional scene to punctuate the end of my epic quest for the Father who will not fail. I won't lie to you—that's kind of the way it always played out in my mind.

Here's how I always thought it would go: seated in the first pew at my Presbyterian church, I would allow God's Spirit to seize me in worship one day. Suddenly, I'd be slain in the Spirit and drop to the floor. I would pick myself up, acting humble but feeling proudly un-Presbyterian, and would proceed to contact each hopeless doctor I had visited with my irresistible testimony. For any doubting Thomas, I would even present my feet for thorough medical inspection. Since all those doctors had the "before" x-rays of my feet, it would not surprise me one bit if I ended up with my own Discovery Channel special, where I could then give my "Good Father" commercial to an even bigger audience! The whole ugly mess would be wrapped up with Hallmark wrapping paper and tied with an award-winning bow. Golly gee, that would have been swell.

For years I had wanted God to magically cure my feet, my heart and my life so that I could merrily scamper out of the lion's den without going through all the cumbersome motions of actually depending on God, rooting my life in God's. In the real world, however, I still had to stretch my feet every morning before I could walk. I still took antidepressants. I still wanted to know my half-siblings, not to mention the father whose genes we wore.

Max Edwards

Max Edwards. I read the name on the guest list for a friend's birthday party I was cohosting with my friend Pam. I made a quick mental note of the interesting fact that some guy in North Carolina had the same name as my birth father and then returned to thinking about tablecloths and wine and tasty desserts.

Most of the revelers had already gathered on my front porch when I heard the phone ring. Though I wasn't feeling particularly chatty, I scurried inside in case a lost guest needed directions. The machine picked up. "This is Max Edwards," a voice began. "I'm trying to find my way . . ."

I grabbed that receiver and tried to speak as if my heart were not thumping out of my chest. "Hello, this is Margot," I began. As the guest-Max continued to describe his location, a few blocks from my home, it slowly dawned on me that he was not, in fact, the Max Edwards for whom my heart beat so quickly. As I hung up, I felt a little disgusted with myself for the rush of adrenaline and hope that had shot through my body.

Returning to those partying on the porch, I regaled them with the amusing story. Friends who know me well chuckled along with me. The ones who didn't weren't sure whether to laugh or cry. When the guest-Max arrived a few minutes later, not one of them mentioned the fact that I, a perfect stranger, had thought for a moment that he might have spawned me. I thought that was very classy of them.

When the phone rang again, the day after the party, I picked it up without screening.

"Hello, this is Max Edwards," a familiar voice began. Like some ridiculous Pavlovian dog, my hungry insides began salivating. Before I could put the pieces together, yet again, the voice added, "I'm not sure if I'm speaking to *Margot* or to *Pam* . . ."

"Um . . ." I stammered, suddenly blank. In that moment *I* didn't know if he was speaking to Margot or to Pam. After an awkward pause for confusion, I remembered both that Max Edwards had been a dinner guest at my home the previous evening *and* that my cohostess shared the same name as my birth mother. He had called to thank us both for a lovely evening.

Rats!

I was not at all thrilled that my heart got excited for that guy. I wished it hadn't. Hanging up the phone, however, I noticed something unusual.

It was silence.

Specifically, there was not the sinister voice in my ear, insisting that I did not merit Max's attention, that I was not worth showing up for and that I deserved to be left.

I knew in my bones that I did, I was and I didn't.

Transforming Truth

Truth, through God's people, was slowly dislodging the lies that my heart had believed. No human voice I'd trusted had ever actually told me I was worthless. None had questioned God's reliability. None had suggested that I'd better armor up to protect myself. I had simply deduced each one from my experience of human absence.

Henri Nouwen, in *The Inner Voice of Love*, describes it this way:

You keep listening to those who seem to reject you. But they never speak about you. They speak about their own limitations. They confess their poverty in the face of your needs and desires. They simply ask for your compassion. They do not say that you are bad, ugly, or despicable. They say only that you are asking for something they cannot give and that they need to get some distance from you to survive emotionally. The sadness is that you perceive their necessary withdrawal as a rejection of you instead of as a call to return home and discover there your true belovedness.*

Jesus had been winding his way through my heart, pausing at each stinging relationship, beckoning in a gentle drawl like the woman at the homeless shelter: "Come in hither. Come and dine." Come home to discover that you are your Father's beloved.

Others

The life-giving assurance that my *real* Father chose to offer himself on the cross, for me, has reordered my relationships. Not only has it affected the way I manage my not-relationship with Max, but it has even affected the relationships in my life that actually exist.

A few months ago I drove to South Carolina to visit an old friend. As we lounged around her home chatting, Maggie mentioned that she'd recently come across an article I'd written about loss that was posted online. In it I mentioned the crippling hurt I once felt when a friend had been late for a movie date. Maggie wondered aloud if it might have been her.

I told her it wasn't. She must not have believed me because she continued on, apologetically, to describe the two times she'd failed me, not showing up on time even though she'd known about my special "issues." Really, now, who doesn't?

---

*Henri J. M. Nouwen, *The Inner Voice of Love* (New York: Doubleday, 1996), p. 13.

I was finally seeing through ick-colored glasses what a treat it must have been to be my friend. It had become painfully clear how the residue of my losses had scummed up our relationship. Yuck.

"It was me, wasn't it?" Maggie asked again nervously.

Looking her in the eye, I used my most persuasive tone to assure her that it was not. Then, breathing a deep sigh of relief, I mused to just myself that it never would be either.

Maggie couldn't tell just by looking at me that I'm different. I don't walk around with a big, goofy grin to let my loved ones know my insides are not quite so devastated anymore. Ironically, now that my fur has been loved off like the Velveteen Rabbit's—now that I'm *real*—I probably smile *less* than I did when I thought my survival depended on it. I can see how it's hard to tell from a not-smile that things are so much better. I should probably wear some kind of sticker or wristband, like a medical alert bracelet. If I did, it might read, "Jesus' Father is *for* me. You too."

Newer friends, of course, don't know the difference. They don't even realize that the person they're dealing with is much more together than I used to be. No one looks at me and thinks, "She's really got her act together."

My new friend Tasha and I were walking through Duke University's campus recently when a little bird hopped by.

"Do you know," she asked, "is that a mockingbird?"

I didn't know what a mockingbird was when I was five and heard about it in the lullaby, and I still don't know now. All I know about birds is that a lot of them look brown and a few jazzy ones are red and blue and yellow.

"Umm," I hedged, wanting to have the right answer but really not having it. "I'm not a bird person, so I can't tell you."

"Hmmm," she mused, staring at it. "I think it is a mockingbird. They're great little songbirds."

Are they now? Fitting, I mused. My dad Rick, who sang barbershop quartet for years, is a great little songbird. He really is. At bedtime, when I was a girl, he always knelt next to my bed and sang me lullabies.

There had been many days since Emily had sung that mockingbird lullaby and prayed for me when Tasha's innocent reference would have sent me spiraling into a very bad place. I wouldn't have flown into a bird-hunting rage, but my insides would have stung. There had been many days that I would have been distracted from the time with my friend, sad for a million unidentifiable reasons. For years I had been raging both against the stupid dad in the lullaby who kept buying horrible gifts, and against the Father of Jesus who seemed to be doing exactly the same thing. I'm even willing to entertain the possibility that I might have been a teensy-weensy bit mad at my own dad. And my biological father. And my ex-stepfather. The whole gang.

When truth had finally sunk into my bones, though, I was freed up to be in relationship with others, each one sinner and songbird. Like me.

Nowadays, if Peter shows up late, rather than crumbling into a quivering mass I remind him, in no uncertain terms, that I am worth showing up for. That really works so much better for both of us.

Lost Stuff

A few months ago I went to Sunday school and, like a big girl, I stayed through the whole class! Our teacher Nick, working through the parables, was teaching the stories Jesus told about a lost sheep, a lost coin and a lost son. Knowing how Bible teachers love to ask people to "find themselves" in the story, I preempted the inevitable suggestion by mentally working ahead.

For years, I mused, I probably would have come up with one of these responses:

I'm not a sheep that's wandered off. Look at me: I'm in Sunday school, for heaven's sake!

Or: *That lost coin is most certainly a Hindu. Maybe Buddhist. Nope, not me.*

Or perhaps: *Well, I probably shouldn't say I'm the* Father *because I know that guy's God, and that seems a little self-important. And I am obviously not a wanton sinner like that really sinful son. I try to be much more discreet with my sinning situations. I'm certainly not that crabby uptight brother. Look at my smile!*

I hadn't been able to see myself in the picture. That was a problem, because the picture was one that Jesus was painting of the Father's great love for his child.

As I daydreamed, Nick continued on, filling in some fascinating facts about shepherds that I never knew. My heart swelling with pity for the lost Hindus, the truth finally hit me like a swift swat from a shepherd's rod. I had been reading the parables, especially the one about the prodigal son, as *prescriptive* rather than *descriptive*.

I had been hearing that story as the doctor-scrawled prescription for salvation. In my ear, it rang as, "I am a wanton sinner, and if I think I'm not—that's a sin. Double bind, see? Sinner! I need to feel really, really guilty. Then, and only then, can I come to my senses and repent, acting surprised, like this guy, that the Father receives me. Even though I already know the story and it won't really be a surprise at all."

Finally, I realized Jesus had simply been *describing* his Dad. Lest you think me terribly insightful, I realized it only because Nick said it. Out loud. At Nick's cue, I began to hear Jesus saying, "I want you to know what my Dad is like. You've all had human experiences of fathers, whether present or absent, and I'm afraid that when I use the word you'll think that mine is like yours. He's not. Let me paint a picture for you of what my Father is like."

Leaning back in my Sunday school chair, I silently decided that it's a shame the way we churchy people have thrown around the word *lost*— like it's a very particular designation for remote tribes of people who go topless, wear loincloths and don't yet have a translation of the New Testament in their language. As if they are the only ones who are "separated" from God.

As Nick continued, it became completely evident that I'd been lost. Lost, as in separated. I had lost parents to relinquishment, a better job, divorce. Far from my real home, I had been separated from the truth of whose I was. I wasn't living there.

Jesus painted all those different pictures of lostness because he didn't want someone like me squinting and muttering, "Mmm, it's just not working for me. I don't really see myself in there." He wanted each sheep and coin, son and daughter, to know that however we have found ourselves lost—to sin or shame, to guilt or depression, to despair or death— the Father longs for us to come home and to discover what he's really like, finding ourselves in the picture of his love.

Finally, I had.

The painting I saw was one of a new Father, beaming with delight, cradling a beloved little girl wearing an orange dress.

Couch Mama

The emerging picture of Jesus' Dad continued to evolve in my imagination. While I'd been pregnant with Zoë, Geni had given me a stuffed animal, a peanut-butter-colored mutt with chocolaty ears and tail, as a shower gift. A tan ribbon had been tied in a bow around Woofie's neck. Geni had pulled me aside at the baby shower to school me in the delicate art of nurturing the bond between child and her luvvy.

"Just take it out of the crib with you when you take the baby out," she instructed firmly. "Carry it with you wherever go. And for the love of all that's sacred, *don't* wash it!" Knowing full well that I had never before bowed to the temptation to launder extraneous household items, she quickly added, "That's why I got you brown."

Sure enough, before she was able to speak, Zoë had bonded with Woofie. Every night Zoë would sniff herself to sleep, Woofie's ribbon woven through her chubby little fingers and shoved partially up one nostril. Woofie quickly became saturated with a nasty yet magical mix of dried slobber, mucus and the faint aroma of stale urine. This, apparently, was irresistible.

Today Woofie is still putting my girl into a Zen-like trance just before bedtime. Despite the fact that Peter and I have begged her to leave Woofie in her room, ignoring Geni's earlier instructions, Zoë doesn't. What this means is that every night, like clockwork, a desperate girl is pillaging our home in search of her lost puppy. Most often Woofie has fallen behind the bed, slid under a chair or flumped off a couch. Sometimes I've scooped Woofie up with the morning laundry. By nightfall that pup may or may not still be in the basket infecting our other textiles. We have even weathered the temporary but devastating loss of Woofie, carelessly dropped during a stroller ride and then camouflaged by wet brown leaves. I suppose it wasn't *wanton* losing, but it sure felt like it. Every single night, Zoë scours our home and van for that puppy.

I care, but not enough to get up off the couch to help her look.

Were Jesus to explain to Zoë what his Father is like, I think he'd do it by telling her a story about Woofie.

Thankfully, he might begin, *my Dad is not like your lazy couch mama. No, here's the thing: my Dad loves you as much as you love Woofie. Cool, huh? If you fall off a bed, my Dad slides his face around your dusty, sticky floor until he finds you. Or, if someone throws you in with the dirty laundry, or hangs you out to dry, you can bet that my Dad takes his flashlight down to the basement, onto the porch, and out into the backyard until he finds you.*

He doesn't rest until he does. Even if you completely disappear from the house and fall into a miry pit of wet leaves, even that is no obstacle for my Dad. He'll scour the neighborhood, the town, the globe until he finds you. That's what my Dad, and yours, is like.

Suddenly, Zoë *gets* it. She understands, in her bones, that she's her Dad's beloved. With a sigh of relief she breathes, "Thank goodness his Dad is not like my mom."

That is a load off my mind too.

Orange

When I'm feeling most like the beloved I know I am now, I actually do wear an orange T-shirt dress. Trimmed at the bottom with lavender flowers, it hangs over my purple-dyed Levis like the colorful two-piece outfits worn by Indian women. I found that comfy dress online about five years ago. When I wear it, I feel like *me*.

I love getting decked out like that princess who God adorned in Ezekiel. I wear a thin rainbow-colored choker necklace that I made, four or five of my favorite earrings, and a sparkly, cubic zirconia nose ring. On my fingers and thumbs are a bunch of silver rings. The right thumb ring is engraved with the word TRUTH. I really wanted LOVE, but LOVE didn't come in my size.

The ring on my left thumb has the words FAITH, HOPE *and* LOVE wrapped around its full circumference. I bought it for the LOVE. The negative space around and inside each letter has been carved out. For years I've used it as a prayer ring. Noticing it on my hand, I spin it to the virtue which seems most needful that day, breathing a prayer to Jesus' Father, and mine, for provision.

There were a lot of years when LOVE and FAITH just didn't see a lot of action. I'm not saying that I had mastered them; it's just that I pretty much needed HOPE *all* the time. During those days I occasionally imagined that, should I be involved in an unfortunate hand fire, my neediness would have been permanently seared on me, scarred into my flesh. Perfect, I mused, since I was always in desperate need of more hope.

In fact, I did pass through the fire of suffering. I lived. I made it, thanks to my tribe. That didn't always seem like a given. I am not without scars, of course. My physical body, my chronically injured feet, still bear them.

Now, though, when I look toward my hand, like an anxious fiancée checking to be sure it's real, the lasting impression I see is LOVE. I'm keenly aware it's not my own.

In the darkest days, faith, hope *and* love had all but been extinguished. Like Israel, I had deduced from my difficult human circumstances that my Father had forsaken me. Hopeless, I had cried out with Zion, "The Lord has forsaken me, my Lord has forgotten me" (Isaiah 49:14).

Straight-faced, the Father asked me,

Can a woman forget her nursing child, or show no compassion for the child of her womb? (Isaiah 49:15)

It sure felt that way.

Even these may forget [the Lord assured me], yet I will not forget you. See, I have inscribed you on the palm of my hands; your walls are continually before me. (Isaiah 49:15-16)

Now God had my attention. My gaze turned from my own hand to notice my Father's. As one might expect, it was a much better view. There I saw my name scarred on his palm. His tattooed hand didn't read *Tama* or *Margot*.

It simply read: *Beloved*.

ACKNOWLEDGMENTS

Because the true stories of God's grace in human lives belong, ultimately, to the church, this story is—in that respect—not my own. Still, I am keenly grateful to my mom, dad and birth mom, Pam, for allowing me the privilege of telling the story we share.

Greg and Cindy, thank you for *seeing* me and hearing—in this story—echoes of the story that is true.

Connect with Margot . . .

at www.theGirlintheOrangeDress.com
or visit her at
www.MargotStarbuck.com
or on Facebook

To invite Margot . . .

to speak to your group,
Visit www.SpeakUpSpeakerServices.com

Learn more . . .

about serving with Urban Promise:
www.UrbanPromiseUSA.org

International Soundex Reunion Registry
www.ISRR.net
P.O. Box 371179
Las Vegas, Nevada 89137

LIKEWISE. *Go and do.*

A man comes across an ancient enemy, beaten and left for dead. He lifts the wounded man onto the back of a donkey and takes him to an inn to tend to the man's recovery. Jesus tells this story and instructs those who are listening to "go and do likewise."

Likewise books explore a compassionate, active faith lived out in real time. When we're skeptical about the status quo, Likewise books challenge us to create culture responsibly. When we're confused about who we are and what we're supposed to be doing, Likewise books help us listen for God's voice. When we're discouraged by the troubled world we've inherited, Likewise books encourage us to hold onto hope.

In this life we will face challenges that demand our response. Likewise books face those challenges with us so we can act on faith.

likewisebooks.com